Cancel Culture:
Tales From The Front Lines

Paul du Quenoy

Cancel Culture:
Tales From The Front Lines

Paul du Quenoy

Academica Press
Washington ~ London

Library of Congress Cataloging-in-Publication Data

Names: du Quenoy, Paul (author)
Title: Cancel culture : tales from the front lines | du Quenoy, Paul
Description: Washington : Academica Press, 2021. | Includes references.
Identifiers: LCCN 2021947823 | ISBN 9781680537529 (hardcover) |
9781680537536 (paperback) | 9781680537543 (e-book)

Copyright 2021 Paul du Quenoy

Contents

Introduction

This collection of essays explores one of the most pernicious developments of our times. Arising from pop culture slang to describe the removal of an undesirable person from one's social ambit, the term "cancel culture" has come into general use for the elimination of an idea, object, creative work, or, indeed, a person thought to be objectionable by individuals or groups who have the informal power to have objects of their disapproval proscribed from public life.

The process is never democratic or in line with the founding principles of our country. Regardless of traditional concepts of liberty and our foundational rights of free speech and expression, an "outrage mob" can form either in person or online and publicly denounce an affront to its sensibilities so great that it must be eliminated, or at the very least subjected to some form of warning or caution establishing that no decent person would tolerate or engage with it.

If this sounds un-American, it certainly should. Our Constitution opposes it in both letter and spirit. Some 64 percent of Americans – including 48 percent of Democrats – believe that "cancel culture" is a serious threat to their personal freedom. Eighty-eight percent identify it as a "problem" of some degree of magnitude, with the largest proportion of respondents – 36 percent – calling it a "big problem." More than half our population worries that expressing a disfavored political opinion could cause them to lose a job, a phenomenon that is hardly unknown. Sixty percent of college students believe they would face negative consequences if they voiced a controversial point of view, while 80 percent of them report having self-censored their speech at least some of the time.

Such fears are far from unfounded. Nearly 90 percent of colleges and universities restrict certain forms of speech and are required by U.S. government administrative directives to investigate and punish broadly defined forms of "discriminatory harassment" with sanctions up to and including expulsion or dismissal. Some 40 percent of millennials favor suppressing free speech that others find "offensive," a higher percentage than in any other demographic group, the older of which have living memories of communism and fascism.

An extraordinary 66 percent of college students believe it is acceptable to shout down a speaker with whom they disagree, while nearly one in four now supports the use of physical violence against someone with an opposing point of view. In some of our nominally best institutions of higher education, violent attacks against controversial speakers have taken place, causing bodily harm and extensive damage, generally without any significant consequences for the perpetrators. The trends suggest that these attitudes are worsening – the 25 percent of college students who support violent action in 2021 represents an increase from 20 percent who felt that way the previous year. As this book goes to press, the Attorney General of the United States has issued a directive instructing the FBI to police public school committee meetings for supposed "threats" and "intimidation," including mere expressions of disagreement with controversial school policies and lesson plans.

Unsurprisingly, proponents of cancel culture try hard to mask both its efficacy and scale. Some deny that it exists at all, while others have attempted to reclassify it as "accountability culture" or "consequence culture," which they believe to be a popular phenomenon that produces sensible outcomes in response to expression that they personally find objectionable or out of step with modern sensibilities (usually as defined by them). Still other apologists have argued that while cancel culture may be real, it is not so very bad in practice since they suppose it affects only a relatively small number of people, and since its victims can sometimes rebound from it. In a jarring paradox, others have even defended cancel culture as itself a manifestation of free speech, including in cases when it disrupts or denies the free speech of others.

Despite these weak and sophistic arguments, there can be little doubt that cancel culture is a real phenomenon and pervasive in our hypersensitive and increasingly polarized public sphere. If it were not real, and a real problem, why have so many people written and worried about it, and why do the arguments of cancel culture deniers sound so ridiculous and even offensive?

This book explores the phenomenon with an eye toward explaining not merely how cancel culture happens but also – and crucially – how it can be resisted. It is brief because the anatomy of cancel culture is simple, as, I believe, is the solution.

In presenting a selection of my own writings over the past year and a half, I have identified sixteen cases of cancel culture across three broad and very important areas – academia, the arts, and popular entertainment – that are relevant to our daily lives and to the general health of our country. I have resisted reproducing mere "outrage copy," texts that decry cancel culture per se, but prefer to look at it as a process. The process always has a discernible beginning – a "call to action" expressed in a public forum. There then follows a reaction to that call to action: an authority figure responds – often anonymously or with little fanfare – in a way that dignifies the call and its motivations. In too many cases, it ends there. The statue is removed, the television show is canceled, the bad man (and it almost always is man) is fired.

It is in the "fallout" that the process becomes interesting. After someone or something is canceled, reactions vary. Sometimes nothing happens at all. Timid professional colleagues of a canceled individual, for example, typically remain silent out of apathy or fear that they may be next. College students with expensive degrees and coveted career paths to worry about often demur from antagonizing their activist peers and the professors and administrators who these days almost always agree with them, or at least say they do. People resisting questionable accusations of racism against others are fully aware that they themselves might be called racists if they speak out. Suburban dissenters are happier to keep their mouths shut rather than risk being thrown out their book clubs and food coops.

On other occasions, only a weak response is offered. Comfortably situated "conservative" columnists might complain in the pages of some "principled" publication and conclude with a comment that they imagine to be witty before straightening their bowties for the next cocktail party at which their Blue State neighbors will tolerate their presence. Tweedy bourgeois types who wish to avoid appearing impolite or guilty of incivility indulge the safe habit of bemoaning the future of the country over private cocktails.

These responses do absolutely nothing to stop cancel culture. They merely signal that cancelation is a fact of life and that its opponents have no real resistance to offer. Cultural hegemony – deciding which forms of expression are acceptable and which are not – is simply ceded to the canceling mob. It is the easy and non-confrontational choice, but it commands no respect and only emboldens the cancelers. If they know they can act with virtual impunity, why should they stop trying to impose their vision of a fair and just society on people who they know will not resist them?

As with any group of bullies, confrontation can stop and reverse cancelation. If a cancel mob forms, a bigger and more vocal gathering can defeat it. If a denounced person's rights are violated, a lawsuit can prove a powerful corrective and impose real consequences. If cancelers are shouting down their victim, shouting back shuts them up. As the courageous actress featured in this book's final essay publicly announced to much acclaim and positive effect for her career, "They can't cancel us if we don't let them." Ultimately, courage is what it takes to resist cancel culture. She clearly has it. Do you?

Section I:
Academia

Don't Kiss Me, Kate:
An Unintended Announcement
of Academia's Irrelevance

In a recent bout of American academia witlessly racing to demonstrate its continuing degradation, Kate Pickering Antonova, an associate professor of history at the ailing City University of New York's Queens College, took to Twitter to unleash bitter invective against six vastly more visible intellectuals who, she feels, "have nothing of value to add and never have," and "produce vapid, superficial, baseless clickbait." This was "not to cancel them," she pleaded immediately after a categorical declaration that "no one should ever publish" them, "ever again," but in fact it was.

Once eliminated, Antonova felt, they and perhaps others like them could be replaced by "THOUSANDS [original capitals] of underemployed adjuncts" with what she believes to be "the education, writing skills, and perspective to contribute SO MUCH MORE [original capitals]."

The intellectuals whom Antonova would like to expel from public life and replace with contingent university instructors of whom she personally approves are the famous journalists Andrew Sullivan and David Brooks, celebrated academics Steven Pinker and Niall Ferguson, and the recognizable internet writers Matt Taibbi and Matt Yglesias. Despite, or perhaps because of, her Columbia University postgraduate humanities education, Antonova did not support her shrill charges against these gentlemen with any empirical evidence – at least not before she temporarily switched her Twitter setting to "protected" as the internet storm clouds began to swell. Nor did she state what the "thousands" of adjuncts she claims to know might contribute from their unidentified "perspective," or how any of it would offer "so much more" than, for example, Pinker's landmark cognitive science studies, which have received nearly 100,000 Google Scholar citations (Antonova, also a tenured full-time university faculty member, appears to have none).

All of those to be purged, however, are cisgendered white males who have recently spoken out against "cancel culture," and all except Sullivan are heterosexual. Sullivan, Brooks, and Ferguson are of the political right (though one might wonder about Brooks), while the others are contrarian liberals who have suffered much worse censure for their unorthodox views than a Twitter screed by an obscure college professor of whom they have no reason to take any notice. In the absence of an argument from Antonova about the content or merits of their work, we might safely assume that she believes these characteristics alone are sufficient to call for them to be denied basic civil rights, just as a large part of our society now seriously believes, and angrily demands that all others recognize, that all white people are racists and that virtually all masculinity is toxic (until recently they also insisted that no woman ever lies about sexual harassment, but that went out the window the second Democratic then-presidential nominee Joe Biden was accused). A fair amount of the academy, where diversity of opinion scarcely exists and is not tolerated if even suspected, likely agrees with her.

But there is more to it. Antonova (an American apparently married to a Russian) is a colleague in my former and now almost moribund academic sub-field, Imperial Russian History. Ironically, given her Twitter outburst, her most visible scholarly work is a book about a nineteenth-century Russian noble family and its evolving sense of the private sphere in a changing society. Back when I still bothered with academia, I was among the relatively small number of people who read it, partly because my wife comes from such a family, but also because the book was tangentially relevant to my own research on a Russian composer and critic who came from a similar social milieu.

More recently, Antonova published a self-proclaimed "essential" guide on how to write historical essays. I have not read that undoubted page turner – and somehow survived 25 years of involvement in university-level history education without consulting her writerly advice – but its presumptuous title suggests that there is only one way (hers) to write history. Antonova also has a viewable blog and Facebook account that largely dwell on the plight of her profession, and particularly of her hard-hit public institution, which is hemorrhaging massive financial loss and seems unlikely to improve at any foreseeable time.

Like the subjects of her scholarly monograph, Antonova is an obvious product of her time and place. Her moribund sub-field sits within the larger academic historical discipline, which is crumbling in popularity and can no longer attract or employ any significant amount of new talent. Following decades of slow decline, the number of undergraduates pursuing history majors in U.S. institutions plummeted by another 50 percent in just the last ten years, in significant part because few students have any use for its off-putting overreliance on abstruse social science theory and the related identity politics nonsense that used to be merely annoying but is now getting people brutalized and killed in American streets.

Even before the economic consequences of Covid-19 devastated academic employment prospects on a mass scale, specializing in history had long since ceased to be a realistic path to virtually any sort of success. Abandoning empiricism rendered it useless for further study in law or any other profession requiring rigorous analytical skills, for which history had long been solid preparation. The remaining mash of critical theory, grievance studies, and social awareness might get the eager young wokeling a job as an activist or community organizer, but he/she/it would be much more inclined to hate the American dream than to live it.

Even the occasional student who simply has an interest in history is now far likelier to track into something more useful and lucrative, particularly since the popular and appealing topics that university-based historians rarely touch – military history, diplomacy, linear political narratives, biographies of "great men," and so on – are booming and increasingly accessible to just about anyone via a wide array of far less expensive and even cost-free formats outside of academia. Indeed, as a former practitioner, I can say with some authority that the best books on Imperial Russia, Antonova's own sub-field, and in many others, are now produced by writers who survive, thrive, and reach far more people than she ever will precisely because they are *not* bogged down by burdensome university affiliations and the heavy baggage that accompanies them, or by the antiquated and highly limited systems of knowledge transmission that date back to the nineteenth century she writes about.

Predictably, history departments like the one in which Antonova teaches at CUNY Queens are among the first to suffer crippling financial cuts, hiring freezes, and general deprioritization by administrators who understandably see ever less value in them every time they review enrolments and look at the bottom line. As an already underfunded public institution deriving more than two-thirds of its budget from the beleaguered coffers of New York State and New York City, the CUNY system is facing an announced reduction of nearly $32 million in public funding next year and has already gone on an adjunct firing spree.

No matter how much Antonova whines on Twitter, many of those adjuncts, whom she would like to elevate to public intellectuals in the place of those non-diverse, cancel culture-resisting males of whom she so obviously disapproves, will no longer be even marginally involved in academia. If there is anyone whom they should blame for their looming para-professional mass extinction as they line up for public assistance or get real estate licenses, it is people like her – arrogant colleagues who think very highly of themselves for no particular reason, made their scholarly fields unappealing and inconsequential, and still have the conceit to turn green with envy over the superior communication skills, social capital, savviness, ambition, and, very often, the far pleasanter personalities that allow non-academic intellectuals to achieve success, fame, and even wealth in articulating their ideas in the public sphere. Antonova may soon be blaming herself for that in a world where even tenured professorships are no longer off the budget cutting table.

SHEAR Madness:
Taking an Old Hickory Switch to the
Dying Academic Historical Profession

Amid the infantile iconoclasm that gripped America after the police killing of George Floyd, the range of targeted monuments even included one of Old Hickory himself, the seventh U.S. president Andrew Jackson. Jackson has long been a loathed figure. A slave owner, he also presided over the forced removal of Cherokee Indians from Tennessee. His frequent resort to duels, irascible character, provocative comments on a range of topics, and demagogic populism have inflicted so many microaggressions on his countrymen living two centuries later that some would prefer to remove him from the nation's past to feel "safe" in its present. A late Obama-era initiative aimed to replace his image on the twenty-dollar bill with that of Harriet Tubman, an organizer of the "underground railroad" that helped slaves escape the antebellum South.

In our fractious era, Jackson has become even more politicized. The Trump administration shelved his replacement on the national currency. When his statue opposite the White House was attacked in June, law enforcement officials swiftly arrested four protesters who tried to topple it and charged them with federal crimes.

A more amusing skirmish in this Jacksonian struggle session has beset something called the Society for Historians of the Early American Republic (SHEAR), an obscure scholarly organization founded in 1977 to facilitate discussion of political history subjects that were being edged out by the historical profession's near-suicidal prioritization of social and cultural history. Yet over the years, the character of SHEAR has also been altered by apparatchiks of academic groupthink to conform to the prevailing party line, not only in the choice of subjects under discussion but also in how they are delivered and by whom.

In 2020, SHEAR's annual conference was postponed due to the Covid-19 pandemic, but its leadership organized an online "plenary panel" over the ubiquitous Zoom. Of course, no one has asked the fundamental question of why, with such technology long available, academia has only now realized that its painful conference rituals are obsolete relics of a mid-nineteenth century intellectual milieu that predated the telephone and the fountain pen (cost-cutting university administrators take note!), but the virtual show went on. On July 17, Daniel Feller, Professor Emeritus at the University of Tennessee and Editor of Andrew Jackson's papers, appeared with a panel of colleague "discussants" (academic duckspeak for "commentators") to present a paper titled "Andrew Jackson in the Age of Trump."

Professor Feller's paper was by no means favorable to the Donald. It criticized the President for claiming Jackson's populist mantle as a forerunner of his own, in part in response to a visit to Jackson's house museum in his home state. But Feller, a self-described Democrat, also warned against overemphasizing Jackson's demerits in order to discredit the current president. Feller characterized this tendency as a form of "historical malpractice" that he believes is perpetrated by journalists and fellow academics, some of whom, it turns out, happen to be (or perhaps we should say "identify as") female, and would do just about anything in their embarrassingly limited power to undermine the president. Feller described this crude enlistment of Early National American history to refract contemporary politics as "indefensible, no matter how noble the cause it purportedly serves."

In normal times, Feller's hedging about a "noble cause" (itself a politically tainted term due its use by the Confederacy in the American Civil War) would have signaled that he is ideologically correct enough to remain an unmolested member of the orthodox clerisy into which his foundering profession has degenerated while nevertheless expressing his personal point of view. Until about two months before the fateful Zoom conference, this had been a relatively uncontroversial act in mainstream American society. His discussants offered their opinions in turn, including some pointed criticisms of Feller's assertions that were not out of line with those one might expect to hear and then just as soon forget at any normal academic conference presentation.

Unhappily for Feller, the virtual format relieved his wider audience of whatever awkwardness might have chilled their bubbling stew of wokeness had they attended his panel in person. In a live format, the retiring academic personality, even when radicalized, tends to demur from abusing a respected elderly colleague to his face.

From a safe digital remove, however, the Zoom comments feature, and the inevitable supplementary discussion on social media, exploded with Red Guard levels of invective. Merely suggesting that his more ideological junior colleagues may have gone too far in demonizing Jackson brought forth strident accusations of "genocide denial." Others angrily castigated as overtly sexist Feller's willingness to critique the work of female scholars who have written on Jackson, one of whom he dared call "incompetent" for the outrageous reason that he believed she was. Still more noted that the panel consisted entirely of white scholars, an unacceptable violation of the diversity shibboleth, even though whites make up an unavoidably overwhelming majority of American history professors.

To make it all worse, toward the end of the session Feller repeated someone else's reference to a dated aphorism holding that Jackson was the nemesis of "redcoats and redskins," the former term indicating the British army in the War of 1812, and the latter a term that Washington's football team until recently used to honor Native Americans. Its use, either in general or in the panel presentation, did not originate with Feller, but he repeated it with the unconscious defiance of a heretic in sixteenth-century Spain, so the inquisitors went to work. Thirty-six of SHEAR's 600 or so members signed an open letter expressing their "outrage" and demanded a "public acknowledgment and condemnation" to correct "the significant damage this behavior has done to the SHEAR community and to others who observed the session." Nobody knows what the other 564 SHEAR members thought, nor has anyone described what this alleged "significant damage" might include.

Within 24 hours, SHEAR's president Douglas Egerton, a noted historian of African-Americans, issued one of those milquetoast apologies in which he acknowledged the complaints about the panel's lack of diversity and engaged in the obligatory cant rejecting racism in all its works and in all its pomps. He did himself in, however, by equivocating that he did not wish to "silence" colleagues with whom he happens to disagree. Smelling blood in his guilt-ridden indecision, all thirteen voting members of SHEAR's "advisory council," including the chairman of Feller's controversial panel, silenced Egerton by "recommending" (that is, "demanding") his resignation, apparently without realizing that his presidency – a one-year elected term – had in fact already ended as scheduled the day before they posted their letter on SHEAR's website.

Not exactly rising to a Jacksonian level of fortitude, Egerton neither pointed out the SHEAR absurdity of their uninformed demand nor stood up for himself or for free speech and inquiry in any other way. Instead, he willing participated in SHEAR's purification ritual by resigning from his automatically conferred new position of "past president" and from SHEAR's executive council. SHEAR's already elected new president Amy Greenberg solemnly declared that she was "grateful to the many scholars who took the time to rightly critique [*sic*] a paper that does not represent either SHEAR's values, or our standards of scholarship" and has courageously pledged to appoint a committee to review SHEAR's "Statement of Values about Anti-Discrimination and Anti-Harassment" to prevent any recurrence of the "many failures" that allowed Professor Feller to exercise his constitutional right of free expression. Her great hope is that her colleagues will conscientiously support her in "earning back and maintaining the trust that has been eroded in our organization and in the public." One might wonder how much of "the public" either knows or cares about her strange sectarian organization, but as an opponent of free expression she has a SHEAR cliff to scale.

An Unfortunate Series of Cancelations:
Cancel Culture Comes To Publishing

On September 30, 2020, Rowman & Littlefield, once a respected American publisher, tersely tweeted that its scholarly imprint, Lexington Books, "has canceled its planned book series 'Problems of Anti-Colonialism' effective immediately." Bruce Gilley, one of its editors and a professor of political science at Portland State University in troubled Portland, Oregon, had an even ruder awakening when he learned that the series's first book, a biography he had written of the forgotten twentieth-century British colonial official Sir Alan Burns, had vanished from Rowman & Littlefield's website just two weeks before it was scheduled to ship in boxes in which printed copies had apparently already been placed. Receiving no explanation in response to inquiries about the book's bizarre disappearance from the publisher's website (at that time it remained listed on Amazon, though noted as "currently unavailable"), Gilley not unreasonably believed that his book had been "canceled" and requested a return of the rights. Rowman & Littlefield apparently obliged.

As an investor with media interests that include a publishing company, I can assure the gentle reader that no publisher ever returns the rights to any book – especially not at the last minute and after months of preparation and publicity costs – unless something is seriously wrong. Just days before this *épopée*, someone called Joshua Mouwafad-Paul, a self-described "Maoist" and "contingent faculty member" who claims to teach philosophy on an adjunct basis at York University in Toronto, and who has published books with titles like *The Communist Necessity*, decided that Gilley's work was not up to snuff and posted a Change.org petition calling on Rowman & Littlefield to eliminate what he called its "shameful" series on anti-colonialism. By the time the petition reached an underwhelming 800 signatures, Rowman & Littlefield canceled the series, allowing Moufawad-Paul to declare victory.

What is the problem with a book series about "problems" of "anti-colonialism?" Apparently, from the point of view of Moufawad-Paul and his supporters, anything that opposes "anti-colonialism" *ipso facto* observes some sort of "good" in colonialism and is therefore unacceptable and even "white nationalist" in perspective. He further accused Gilley of being unqualified to write about colonial history, though Moufawad-Paul himself appears to have no training of any kind in History, Africa, colonialism, the British Empire, or anything other relevant subject. Tellingly, Moufawad-Paul also noted that Rowman & Littlefield previously published a number of "anti-colonial" scholars and argued that no honest publisher could produce work that might disagree with theirs. The groupthink's orthodoxy runs rampant, but hardly anyone has observed the grating and most colonial irony that a subject of Her Majesty the Queen effectively caused the cancelation of an American publication.

Gilley's cancelation quickly went viral, with sympathetic articles appearing in the London *Times* and elsewhere. Two senior scholars who endorsed his book affirmed its quality and bemoaned his critics. Gilley himself took to Twitter, where he compared Moufawad-Paul and his supporters to the Taliban, and to the *Wall Street Journal*, in which he published a lengthy op-ed bewailing his fate and calling for more freedom and diversity of opinion in his toxic profession. A rival online petition collected more than four thousand signatures to vindicate Gilley's scholarly reputation and called upon Rowman & Littlefield to apologize. As of this writing it has not done so, but rather maintained, however unconvincingly, that its removal of Gilley's book from its website was merely for "review" purposes, and that the series was canceled only because there were allegedly no other books yet submitted in it. Speaking again as a publisher and former academic, this is the first time I have ever such a reason advanced to cancel a book series.

But hope and good fortune arrived. Gilley himself hinted at a silver lining in his *Wall Street Journal* op-ed, confessing a "ghoulish satisfaction" in the vastly greater publicity the scandal would bestow upon an otherwise obscure book by an obscure college professor about an obscure colonial official. Prior to the cancelation, a scholarly biography of this type might have attracted tens of readers or fewer. Now it might get a few hundred.

Gilley's foresight was justified. Having read his op-ed, and subsequently encouraged by the Free Speech Union, I immediately stepped forward with an offer to publish his book within three months of the cancelation, just as my company last year picked up and quickly published the intelligence researcher James R. Flynn's book on free speech and universities after its original British publisher dropped it at the last minute for purported legal reasons. I also offered to adopt the rest of Gilley's canceled series, assuring him that I never have been and never will be moved by cancel culture or the revolting sensibilities that enable it. After receiving and verbally agreeing on a contract, however, Gilley decided to go with another publisher, though at least one other book in the series has been published by me. In today's climate, however, scholars like Gilley are rapidly running out of welcoming homes.

A Pigment of Her Imagination:
The Pitfalls of (Not) Being
Black in American Academia

George Washington University, my undergraduate alma mater, sprawls across official Washington, DC, occupying much of a historic but overrun neighborhood unpromisingly called "Foggy Bottom." Situated between the White House and the State Department, its western edge faces leafy Georgetown, home to my graduate alma mater, while its eastern fringes dissolve into downtown, now for the most part boarded up and eerily abandoned after all those "largely peaceful" race riots we heard about in the months since George Floyd's killing in June 2020.

GW, as it is locally known, is now itself at the center of a bizarre race drama that has captured international headlines. On September 3, Professor Jessica A. Krug of the university's history department, where I studied for my BA and where she came to teach Africana studies about 15 years later, posted a maudlin confession on the open-platform website Medium. After having presented herself for most of her adult life variously as African-American, Afro-Caribbean, Afro-Latina, an "El Barrio" community member, an "unrepentant and unreformed child of the hood," or, as we are now allowed to say again, just plain black, she admitted that it was all a fraud. As she melodramatically put it, her deception was "the very epitome of violence, of thievery and appropriation." The charade was "unethical, immoral, anti-Black [*sic*], [and] colonial," she continued, blaming long-term mental health issues caused by alleged childhood abuse for her decision to mask her true heritage, which is white, Jewish, and the product of suburban Kansas City.

Denouncing herself as a "coward" and "culture leech," Krug offered no apology, arguing that there was no excuse for her imposture or any possible recompense for the damage she believes it has caused. Instead, she insisted that she should be "canceled" by a "cancel culture" that she claims to support, and even offered to "cancel" herself, perhaps to spare the woke world the trouble.

The woke world held its delicate breath for a moment and then blew out a hurricane of invective. Social media erupted with angry and wounded condemnation. Friends, colleagues, and students outdid each other denouncing Krug for what they regard as a personal betrayal, a violation of professional trust, the "destabilization" of her academic field, unspecified "harm" to minorities everywhere, "cultural appropriation," "minstrelsy," and the basest hypocrisy. One said he couldn't sleep because of her revelation. GW's administration almost immediately announced that it was "looking into the situation" and later confirmed that Krug would not be teaching in Fall 2020, pending an investigation. It added a mandatory formulation about recognizing the "pain" she has allegedly caused, and promised to provide institutionally-sponsored counseling to anyone who simply cannot get over the trauma of living a world in which Jessica A. Krug is, in fact, white.

One day after Krug's confession, GW's history department prominently posted "Our Statement on Jessica Krug." It professed that "the members of the faculty" were "shocked and appalled" that she had "betrayed the trust of countless current and former students, fellow scholars of Africana Studies, colleagues in our department and throughout the historical discipline, as well as community activists in New York City and beyond," and that she had thereby "raised questions about the veracity of her own research and teaching." Although GW's investigation had not yet begun – and despite the plain fact that any of the "questions" that may have been "raised" by Krug's strange conduct have yet to be asked let alone answered, – she was to be shown no mercy. "The department calls upon Dr. Krug to resign from her position as associate professor of History at GW," the department's statement concluded. "Failing that, the department recommends the rescinding of her tenure and the termination of her appointment." Under enormous pressure, Krug resigned a few days later. Her larger fate is unknown.

The language of the GW history department's statement suggested a unanimous opinion, but one of its senior faculty members told me that he was not consulted about the matter. Remembering some of his colleagues, and having spent half my life in academic environments that cannot be described as either speedy or efficient, it seems highly unlikely that GW's 36 other full-time history professors discussed, drafted, unanimously voted for, and then published the statement in just one day in pandemic conditions at the end of the first week of a new and deeply troubled academic year. Nevertheless, whoever approved the statement really meant it – a link to it posted on Twitter was the department's first tweet in almost three years, and a tab leading to it has been added to its website, alongside the tabs for "About" and "People."

As an alumnus, I am profoundly grateful to GW for parodying contemporary academia so brilliantly that we now have this treasure trove of material for the ingenious satire that begs to be written about this. Let us start with the obvious fact that no one else seems willing to address: Jessica Krug actually looks like a white woman. She has been accused of playing up her minority persona in speech, dress, and style – and has mastered the ideological language of an aggrieved minority with intellectual pretensions, – but endless photos of her from various stages of her adult life would lead no reasonable person to conclude anything other than that she is white. Close family members, some of whom have spoken to the media, remember her as a definitely white woman and were astonished to learn that she had assumed a different racial identity.

But what might be astonishing in suburban Kansas, or in any other cognitively normal environment, has become the norm in American academia, where the requisite "sensitivity" – now the nearly universal subject of mandatory "training" – bars the questioning of any individual's personal identities and characteristics, including even neutral inquiries about what they factually are. Already an awkward Larry David-esque thing to be avoided, many details one might question, including race, are "protected" by civil rights laws that universities must rigorously enforce on pain of legal action, investigation by the U.S. Department of Education, and possible loss of US federal government funds.

In practice, that means that if a white woman tells you she is black in a university setting, you cannot so much as look at her skeptically without risking a discriminatory harassment complaint, which official institutional policies not only encourage her to make but also require any third party aware of the exchange to report even if the woman does not want to complain. You will then face a thorough investigation by an administrator and perhaps a panel of faculty members, none of whom usually has any legal training, but all of whom voluntarily chose to dedicate an enormous amount of their time and energy to exercising potentially career-ending power over their colleagues.

These delightful individuals have received undisclosed additional "training," which instructs them that discriminatory harassment is a problem of catastrophic proportions and that most people – especially women and minorities – virtually never lie about having suffered it. So oriented, your inquisitors will almost certainly presume that you are a racist or some other kind of miscreant and spend weeks or even months combing through your personal and professional life for any corroborating hint of that presumption. About 75 percent of the time – identical to the percentage of defendants declared guilty by the Revolutionary Tribunal of France during the Terror, – they will find that you are "responsible" (i.e. "guilty") for having violated a strict non-discrimination policy and should be sanctioned with disciplinary action. Even if you are among the minority of respondents who are cleared as "not responsible" (i.e. "innocent"), the mere accusation often ricochets in reputational consequences and serious professional fallout. Witness the hysterical calls before GW's investigation even began for Krug's own immediate defenestration for allegedly crossing a racial line, and her stigmatizing exclusion from teaching while that investigation was to take place.

With this Sword of Damocles hanging menacingly over everyone's head, when meeting someone like Jessica Krug it is much easier and safer simply to believe the lie, however obvious or absurd it may be. The potential consequences of even casually questioning it are simply too great and far outweigh any possible benefit, which would usually amount to little more than satisfying mild curiosity about an individual known in the workplace. The only time I recall reacting to someone's questionable workplace self-presentation in my own abandoned academic career involved an involuntary chuckle at a deeply insecure Egyptian colleague's doubtful claim of illegitimate Habsburg descent. I quickly forgot the incident, only to have her rebuke me for it two years later, telling me how very offended she had been. We never spoke again – *Franz Josef sei Dank*, – but I have had occasion to share the tale with real Habsburgs, who found it as hilarious as her claims were preposterous.

My Cairene microaggression notwithstanding, who today could imagine calling out a black professor who decided to "pass" as white, or a professor of Jewish heritage who chose to identify as a gentile, to say nothing of the terrible risks that flow from using the wrong pronoun for an individual who claims, in defiance of any physical evidence, to be transgendered? In Krug's experience, it seems no one ever called her out, including any of her GW colleagues who immediately wanted her head *hors enquête* after having hired, promoted, tenured, and for eight years shared collegial space with her without registering any notice of her deception.

Perhaps unsurprisingly, the best explanation of why Krug suddenly confessed appears to be that a couple of curious colleagues in her scholarly field outside GW began to wonder about her earlier in 2020, after it was revealed that a recently deceased writer interested in Latin American identity, who claimed to be a Cuban childhood immigrant, was in fact an African-American from Detroit with no Caribbean roots. Others seem to have broken academic taboo, at least to themselves or among very close colleagues, to raise questions about Krug's skin color, mainly to observe that she did not strike them as "black enough" to be who she said she was. A self-described "former friend" of hers announced that she was about to be exposed as a *poseuse* and further posited that she had confessed on Medium to mitigate the damage. Like her situational antecedents among the hapless Bolsheviks who fell victim to Stalin's purges, Krug may have imagined that confession and public self-criticism would spare her a worse fate. But also like them, it very well might not.

Krug is clearly an odd and deeply disturbed woman of questionable character, little integrity, and an uncertain grasp of reality. But none of this ever barred her from successful academic employment. If it did, our Ivory Towers would rapidly empty out. Despite the outrage, all her critics really have on her is that she lied about her race in a way that hurt people's feelings. No one has presented any evidence suggesting that her deception tainted or invalidated her academic work, which appears to be about disparate African ethnic communities that formed a hybrid society to resist colonialism and enslavement. Her doctoral dissertation and Duke University Press book on that subject, which was supported by a prestigious Fulbright-Hays fellowship and was almost certainly the basis of her promotion and tenure at GW, was widely praised by respected scholars and selected as a finalist for two distinguished book awards in her field (Duke University Press later pledged to donate all proceeds from Krug's book to a fund to support minority scholarship). If GW had stripped her of tenure and fired her simply because she falsely told people she was something other than white, she would have had a solid civil rights lawsuit in which she could easily have invoked freedom of expression and association, and probably also brought convincing due process and breach of contract claims. If, on the other hand, GW revealed that it hired Krug *because* it understood her to be a minority, then any white candidate for her position who was denied employment could credibly sue for discrimination. This may well be why some people in her department wanted her to go immediately and of her own volition, which she obligingly did. But perhaps they might have taken a break from the hysteria that made capital fools of them to consider whether it would be better if race were no longer a category of consideration in professional hiring.

Saving Professor Flynn:
In Memory of a Scholar and Free Speech Advocate

"Its publication, in particular in the United Kingdom, would raise serious concerns. By the nature of its subject matter, the work addresses sensitive topics of race, religion, and gender … it is with regret that [we have] taken the decision not to publish your manuscript." So did James R. Flynn, the eminent political philosopher and scholar of intelligence research who died on December 11, 2020, at age 86, learn that his book, originally titled *In Defence of Free Speech: The University as Censor*, had been canceled by a British publisher that had reviewed it, accepted it, and even advertised its imminent release in a catalogue that it had embarrassingly printed just before the cancelation. The situation's absurdity was even more readily apparent than the usual run-of-the-mill cancelation stories that we now hear almost daily. This was not a book by an obscure professor on an abstruse academic topic that had proved incendiary for some marginal reason; this was a book by an internationally recognized scholar of major repute about the foundational principle of free speech itself, and that fundamental human right's sad fate in our institutions of higher education. Several months later the book appeared under its new title, *A Book Too Risky To Publish: Free Speech and Universities*, with Academica Press, which my lot in life is to own. At Professor Flynn's suggestion, the book's cover shows a missile marked "Speech Code" rocketing toward a generic neo-Gothic edifice that could be almost any established university.

Jim was no stranger to free speech issues. A lifelong man of the left who once belonged to America's Socialist Party, his early academic career had been bedeviled by hidebound administrators in the United States. He was twice fired from university posts for speaking out in defense of intellectual freedom and civil rights. Finding the early 1960s American intellectual scene oppressive, he emigrated to New Zealand, where he taught at the University of Canterbury before becoming a professor at the University of Otago, from which he retired last year. Although he was a philosopher by training, he built a distinguished academic career studying the more scientific phenomenon of human intelligence.

This research focus proved fundamental in Jim's late-life trouble, for it inevitably involved participation in decades-long debates over the relationship between intelligence and race. Jim did not believe that there was any genetic correlation between race and intelligence, but rather argued that intelligence is shaped by environmental factors that tend to correlate with the socio-economic status of social groups, including groups defined by race. A logical corollary of that assertion is that when a group's socio-economic conditions improve, average intelligence within that group correspondingly rises.

Jim's empirical research strongly supported that conclusion. Indeed, an entire concept known in cognitive science as the "Flynn Effect" derived from Jim's broad observation that material improvements in the human condition have caused a substantial increase in human intelligence across the board. Taken over a century, he found that average intelligence today would have rated at near-genius levels a hundred years ago, while average intelligence a hundred years ago would rate at borderline developmentally disabled levels today. This rise was simply too fast and too dramatic to be explained by genetic change or natural selection – processes that takes eons rather than decades, – while marked short-term rises in intelligence among historically disadvantaged groups have occurred alongside rapid improvements in environmental factors that benefit intelligence.

Interacting with those who posited or, more accurately, were accused of positing a racial or related genetic component in variations of intelligence exposed Jim to brutal assaults against his colleagues, particularly the social scientist Charles Murray, whose work has been mischaracterized as racist and eugenicist. In 2017 Murray's invited appearance at Middlebury College ended in a violent confrontation that shut down his guest lecture and concussed the unfortunate professor who invited him.

In those simpler times, the verb "to cancel" was not yet applied to people, but what happened to Murray at Middlebury presaged much of what Anglospheric intellectual life has suffered since, right down to Jim's cancelation two-and-a-half years later. Jim was rightly horrified by what happened to Murray; the episode is the subject of an entire chapter of his book. More recently, we have seen the same phenomenon unfold in the vaporization of others, including academics, authors, editors, journalists, politicians, cultural personalities, business leaders, and even long dead historical figures whose views as stated, or even merely as interpreted, have offended some modish sensibility among the militantly woke of 2020. Drawing on arcane critical theorists, many of whom later repudiated their own work, those militants have tried hard to recast free speech and free inquiry, along with logic, rhetoric, grammar, and even good manners and correct attire, as tools of oppression that should be undermined or done away with, unless, of course they are the ones talking.

Jim worked in science, which he regarded as a long-extended "holiday" from his work in philosophy, but he was a man of principle before all else. He firmly believed that the best way to deal with an opponent with whom one disagreed – as he disagreed with Murray and others in his field – was simply to present a better and more persuasive argument, regardless of the subject. Ousting opponents from public discourse, whether by "deplatforming" disfavored ideas, "canceling" them and their work, resorting to physical violence or intimidation, or, needless to say, refusing to publish their books, smacked uncomfortably of the authoritarianism he had suffered as a young academic. By the time of his book's cancelation, this point of view placed him decidedly, if not for him comfortably, on the right, at least in cultural politics. Despite having in effect been a liberal who was "mugged by reality" when his book was canceled, he still preferred to maintain an independent posture. He wondered, for example, if today's right-wing paladins of free speech would maintain their principles if they ever recover the intellectual high ground, or if they would merely disregard free speech and impose their own orthodoxies with the same rigidity of today's leftist commissars.

Jim wrote about his canceled book in a frank and very moving piece in *Quillette* just after it happened. By discussing his misfortune in a popular forum, he did the best possible thing. He exposed the false logic and bullying tactics of his persecutors for what they are. He did not hide from the pall of controversy and blithely take his lumps in the naïve belief that Anglo-American academia had his best interests at heart. He did not debase himself in a degrading apology ritual to express sorrow to those whom his views may have hurt or display contrition before those who sought to humiliate or even destroy him. He shed no tears to bait his cancelers to attack him further. He did what had caused him so much trouble 60 years before but gave birth to a career that lasted a lifetime – he spoke out.

And he won. Dozens of high-profile colleagues publicly defended Jim, including Charles Murray and the Harvard psychologist Steven Pinker, both of whom glowingly endorsed his book as "invaluable" and "essential." In March 2021, Murray discussed it along with me and the similarly embattled University of Pennsylvania law professor Amy Wax in an online event hosted by the National Association of Scholars. Pinker, whose magnum opus is a compelling defense of the Enlightenment, recently eulogized Jim as a "defender of Enlightenment ideals." The *New York Times*, once the paper of record but hardly the heartiest defender of free speech these days, honored him with a lengthy and laudatory obituary. Even Jim's original British publisher shamefacedly "liked" our Academica Press Twitter post announcing his book's publication.

After Jim's *Quillette* article appeared, he received offers from no fewer than fifteen publishers, all of whom were eager to rescue his canceled book. When my house released it in the final days of 2019, it attracted much positive attention but no adverse criticism of which I am aware. There was no attempt to silence Jim in the remaining year of his life, and there has been no pressure on my company or on me to withdraw, modify, or otherwise diminish his book, which continues to attract considerable international attention. If there were, we would promptly tell any bumptious critics what to go do with themselves and then, following Jim's sterling example, expose them for the cheap bullies they are. This, more than anything, is how cancel culture will lose. Bullies, when resisted, are fundamentally cowards who will back down, disappear, or simply become irrelevant before the resolve of their would-be victims. Like any tyranny, theirs cannot withstand ridicule. All free speech proponents need is courage backed by the comforting realization that they are not alone.

Several of the presses Jim turned down were right-wing outfits that he feared would weaponize his book to score political points in our new culture wars and cause it to be tarred as propaganda for the Trumpian hordes. Indeed, books released by such publishers frequently do suffer that fate, or are simply ignored. All too often, their logos are practically bullseye targets that cause serious and thoughtful writers to be accused of every kind of social and ideological misdeed and excluded from mainstream public discourse. This is, of course, the opposite of what Jim believed in and of what Academica Press, which has no political orientation, proudly supports – an open and uncensored society in which debate and disagreement flourish in the pursuit of truth. By standing up to his bullies, Professor Flynn helped restore that ideal and has already encouraged others to do so. May he rest in peace.

Section II:
The Arts

Trouble in Tahiti:
Paul Gauguin's works at
the National Gallery of Art, London

"Is It Time Gauguin Got Canceled?" barked the title of an appallingly serious recent article in the *New York Times*. Anyone who saw a recent exhibit of Paul Gauguin's portraits at London's National Gallery of Art[1] and made the mistake of reading the commentary might be forgiven for righteous agreement with the erstwhile paper of record. Far from celebrating the artist's sensual flight from the limitations of an industrialized bourgeois Europe, the commentary instead instructed the viewer that Gauguin's most intriguing work – his "sometimes troubling" (uh oh!) Polynesian period – was merely an indulgence in "colonial and misogynist fantasies" of a place where he "undoubtedly exploited his position as a privileged Westerner to make the most of the sexual freedoms available to him." The exhibit's audio guide echoes the point even more bluntly, musing in a condescending schoolmarm's tone whether it is time for us prurient children to stop looking at Gauguin's work altogether, presumably before the Torquemadas of Title IX strike it from university curricula to spare milquetoast millennials from yet another of life's cruel triggers.

The unimpeachably woke credentials of whoever wrote the exhibit's nonsensical commentary stand out like an ousted Stalinist Labour MP in a United Kingdom where the national political party of wokeness suffered its worst electoral defeat since 1935 while the exhibition was on. Gauguin lived most of his life in extreme poverty, however, and neither had nor expected "privilege" in the South Seas. He went there after failing to find any other place original enough to inspire his creative impulses – a list that included the culturally distinct Brittany of his native France, the Peru of his childhood, and the Caribbean wanderings of his early adulthood. His work from his Polynesian years, along with his attempts to popularize Polynesia as the origin of a chic new

---

[1] "Gauguin Portraits," National Gallery, London, October 7, 2019-Jannuary 26, 2020.

style, flopped in a Europe that knew virtually nothing about a place that would hardly be thought of, and still less "exoticized," in the mainstream West for at least another half century.

Noa Noa, the artist's short journal of Polynesian life whose title means "fragrant scent," is replete with soulful gratitude for generosity extended in a beautiful place where Gauguin settled as a warmly received guest enjoying the hospitality with which any visitor to those beautiful islands is showered. This extended to Polynesia's sexual freedoms, which gave him two wives who would today be legal minors but who were not dramatically younger than the teenage brides Europe regularly produced in the era. France's age of consent at the time was thirteen; today it is fifteen. And, in perhaps the ultimate irony for the National Gallery's white male bashers whose experience of Polynesia probably does not extend beyond overly sweetened cocktails at some Shoreditch hellhole, Gauguin's final years saw him become a vehement opponent of colonial rule.

One of the few disappointments for those of us who actually have been to French Polynesia is the absence of Gauguin's work from the setting in which he created it. Tahiti's local Gauguin Museum contains only reproductions of works now held in European and American collections. Portraits selected from among these works form the core of the exhibit and they are glowing, no matter how "problematic" the curators tried to make them in their asinine scribblings.

Charmingly presented against a background of warm colors in London's cold, damp winter, the exhibit embraces multiple media to show how Gauguin perceived the human image. It begins with his earliest experiments from his mid-thirties, when he determined to become a full-time artist, in a series of self-portraits depicting himself in guises ranging from self-assured artist he hoped to be to poses as a suffering Christ in dramatic New Testament scenes. More than mere narcissism, their aim, following the self-portrait mastery of Dürer and Rembrandt, was to express a worldview defined by the artist as subject. Having mastered rendering his own facial expression, Gauguin moved on to Parisian subjects, exemplified by his 1884 portrait of his Danish first wife Mette

Gad, whose swirling evening dress and angular bearing would have made her a fit subject for Manet.

Not content with what could easily have become mannered portraits of Parisian socialites, Gauguin wandered off to Brittany to paint its local people in their distinctive garb. The portraits became more abstract in their geometry ("primitives," as he described them), in a manner that anticipated Matisse, Picasso, and Braque. He still managed to insert a self-portrait in this idiom, featured in 1889's *Bonjour, Monsieur Gauguin*. Painting briefly in the tempestuous company of Vincent van Gogh in the "Studio of the South" in the southern French city of Arles, its uses of light and symbol became more prominent before Gauguin determined to embark for Polynesia.

Having exhausted other distant locales, Polynesia was a radical yet natural choice. Only colonized in 1880, it had experienced just over a decade of French rule by the time Gauguin arrived in 1891. In a carved up world of empires, it remained "unspoiled" enough for the artist's sensibilities while remaining prudently French-speaking for his practical needs and drenched in sunlight for his innovative adaptation of light.

His early portraits there, such as *Woman of the Mango* (1892), depicted local women in the newly introduced long dresses that nettlesome missionaries had introduced out of concern for the modesty of their new converts. Gauguin detested this sartorial colonialism and quickly began to paint them in their traditional affect, but in the stylized idiom of his new approach. *Exotic Eve*, from the first half of the 1890s, presents a nude in an approximation of the Garden of Eden, a religious reference that captured the artist's almost mystical attitude toward his new home (after a failed return to France, Gauguin returned to Polynesia in 1895 and remained there until his death in 1903). *Barbarian Tales* (1902) includes a crouching self-portrait staring forward in contemplation past two cross-legged bare breasted women with only skimpy bands about the waist and flowers crowing their hair.

Marquesas Man in the Red Cape (or *The Sorcerer of Hiva Oa*), also from 1902, incorporates a sharp red cape and sacred animals in the best traditions of European aristocratic portraiture to depict the endurance of native traditions in the face of the colonial rule Gauguin despised. It was likely no accident that his sculptured wood portraits include an irreverent depiction of the lecherous missionary bishop Monseigneur Martin, who castigated Gauguin for his relationships with native girls while carrying on several of his own, as "Père Paillard," or "Father Lechery" (1902). This primitive visage captured the hypocritical cleric as a naked devil with horns prominently protruding from his oversized head. Martin was unamused when Gauguin displayed the carving in front of his final place of residence to show the passing Polynesians exactly what he thought to their local mission priest, but he did not have to stomach Gauguin much longer. The artist died just a year later, at the age of 54. He may have been broke, but at least he was not woke.

Dancing Degas:
"Degas at the Opéra" at
the National Gallery of Art, Washington

Downtown Washington, DC has been a ghost town for quite some time, with virtually the entire federal government and supporting professional workforce long ago sent home by the pandemic and all those "largely peaceful protests." The Smithsonian museums long remained closed, but the National Gallery, situated among them yet a distinct entity, cautiously reopened to the general public on July 20, 2020. Its reopening was subject to masks and limited timed entry slots, but it allowed for a renewed run of this exhibition of works by Edgar Degas (1834-1917), which originally opened on March 1 and lasted only a short while before Covid-19 closed everything down.[2]

The exhibition's title is a bit deceptive. Its subject is not Degas's impressions of opera as an art form, but rather his creative work in and around the milieu of Paris's *Opéra*, the French capital's storied performing arts institution. Historically, the *Opéra* has presented both opera and ballet, the latter of which interested Degas far more even though ballet was in decline relative to opera for most of his adult lifetime. Shared with Paris's Musée d'Orsay, which mounted this exhibition in late 2019 to celebrate the 350th anniversary of the *Opéra's* founding, it mainly features works from American collections, including a large number from the National Gallery itself. They chronicle in illuminating detail Degas's interest in less visible aspects of the theatrical experience – rehearsals, backstage drama, actions in the wings, the orchestral musicians, the audience, and other perspectives that the artist observed, remembered, or, as was often the case, imagined.

The exhibition opens with a seminal work, Degas's painting of a dance sequence that occurs within an opera, *The Ballet from "Robert le Diable"* (1871-1872), the titular opera by Giacomo Meyerbeer composed

---

[2] "Degas at the Opera," National Gallery of Art (Washington), March 1, 2020-October 12, 2020

in the French "grand opera" style that required a ballet. This canvas reflects Degas's attraction to the contrast of performance and audience. The bottom third of the painting depicts an all-male group of spectators who are mostly ignoring the action on stage, a dance sequence for a cast of possessed nuns. The most prominent figure among the spectators is a middle-aged man pointedly looking through his opera glasses away from the stage and up at the boxes and, presumably, at the female spectators therein. The nuns, dressed in white, are vividly juxtaposed in a motion sweeping enough to obscure the line of their figures, which Degas executed in neater brush and sepia studies (presented alongside the painting) and then abstracted.

Degas's interest in the human surroundings of performance radiates in a number of other works. His *Portrait of Eugénie Fiocre* (1867) depicts that leading dancer in the principal role of Léo Délibes and Ludwig Minkus's ballet *La Source*, but eschews any depiction of dance or character in favor of a sumptuous portrait of Fiocre simply looking wan and tired in exotic costume. An homage more to the woman than to her art form, it precedes a room of containing *The Orchestra of the Opéra* (1870), which foregrounds the ensemble of musicians while limiting the view of the stage to the pink tutus of the dancers, whose heads fall above the frame. In a moment of personal license, Degas imaginatively rearranged the orchestra to reduce it in size, place the musicians in profile rather than facing away from the spectator, and to center his friend, the bassoonist Désiré Dihau, where the concert master, always a violinist, should be. This celebration of the milieu also features the composer Emmanuel Chabrier peering out of a box.

The world of performers beyond the idolization of fandom also captivated Degas. Rehearsals were not open to the general public or to him, either as an artist or as a ballet subscriber, but his imagination and some studio studies allowed him to produce evocative paintings of ballet in preparation. The actions and events are stylized, but his mind ran toward work-in-progress aspects of the art form. Such paintings as the aptly named *The Rehearsal* (1874) and *Dancer Adjusting Her Slipper* (1884) present unvarnished views of awkwardness in movement, with poses and footwork veering less toward the perfection at which instruction aimed than toward awkwardness and error inevitability encountered on that path. The surrounding studies, done in pastel, illustrate movements down to flexes of muscle that Degas later stylized in the paintings. His series of elongated panels and decorative fans telescope the figures and their environments in panoramas that recall the much larger processional masterpieces of the Italian Renaissance in their representation of figures serially deployed to create a larger scene. In the seminal *The Dance Class* (1875-1876), among other works, Degas imagines the *Opéra's* longtime ballet master Jules Perrot nostalgically presiding over them, even though Perrot's association with the theater preceded Degas's major working period by several decades.

Perhaps the most striking example comes at the end of the exhibit, in Degas's sculpture *Little Dancer Aged Fourteen* (1878-1881), a remarkably ugly image of the ballet pupil Marie van Goethem, who was dismissed from her studies for poor conduct and frequent absences and, never having mastered the graceful movements required by her art form, offered a model for the raw and unfinished qualities that Degas sought to convey in painting. Derided as hideous as its unveiling, *Little Dancer* and the story behind it developed a sort of cult following and were even the subject of a new ballet staged by the *Opéra* in 2010 (video on display).

The stage itself emerged in unusual perspectives that Degas came to privilege. *Before Curtain-Rise* (1892), done in pastel on paper, looks down at an angle on the last moments prior to the curtain going up, when a dresser whose work resembles genuflection puts the final touches on a dancer's bright green costume. *The Star* (1876-1877) shows a prima ballerina in the throes of movement, but as she would be scene from a slightly elevated box at just above stage right. Here a pale white light radiates the figure in a preternatural shade suggesting moonlight as visible spectators in the wings enjoy their own unique perspective of her. *Dancer Readjusting Her Strap* (1889) captures backstage intimacy in a ballerina's nervous attention to her costume as a colleague in front of her motions forward to perform.

As Degas encountered impressionism later in his career, he nodded to the newer school with what he called "orgies of color," larger scale pastel works featuring flatter forms, deeper textures, and bolder and more vibrant hues. *Four Dancers* (1899) adapts the awkward off-stage motions of anticipation and nervousness familiar from his earlier *oeuvre* to a newer perceptive truth – that the dancers are not individuals but a swaying mass of undifferentiated femininity. As though to pay recently accrued artistic debts, the painting features backgrounded haystacks that acknowledge Monet's influence. Degas's earlier *Portrait of Rose Caron* (1892) stylizes and even obscures the features of its subject, a famous dramatic soprano for whom Degas wrote a sonnet, among other intimacies, and emphasizes her pale, elongated arms as she reclines while sliding on a glove.

If the exhibition was probably more interesting to its French spectators, who had less access to American-owned works, than to American patrons aware of Degas's considerable presence in collections in their country, it certainly has an axe to grind. From the first explanatory panel, we are warned that Degas included "dark suited 'subscribers' (male season ticket holders) lurking in the wings." "These wealthy and powerful men," the text alerts us, "were allowed backstage where they could prey upon the young ballerinas whose poverty and inferior social position made them vulnerable to exploitation."

The text ignores that Degas himself became a ballet subscriber in 1885, and was thus one of the evil old rich men he is imagined to have castigated in his art. But no evidence suggests that he engaged in any amount of criticism of himself, his fellow subscribers, or their alleged behavior, as the exhibition would have us believe. Its introduction to French theatrical life is thus, to borrow an already worn out woke cliché, "problematic." It also seems a bit anachronistic. The text was almost certainly written prior to the Musée d'Orsay's mounting of the exhibition last year, when we were still in peak #MeToo. Frozen in time by the pandemic, even if only for a few months, it missed the shift from sexual harassment accusations to implications of racism as our society's principal dog whistle for social and cultural transgression. Indeed, in light of the wokesters' recent pivot to fervent anti-racism, which is sweeping the art world as relentlessly as any other institutional environment, the exhibition's opprobrium of "predatory" dark male figures "lurking" to "prey upon" young white women could well invite censure in post-George Floyd America.

Perhaps more importantly, the exhibition commentary stands out in stunning ignorance of the realities of nineteenth-century theatrical culture. Backstage attachments certainly happened, but I am unaware of even one case in which a ballerina ever registered a complaint or regret about suffering "exploitation" at the hands of one of her admirers, many of whose attachments were chaste and even unspoken. There are, however, many famous cases, then and now, in which ambitious women cultivated, consented to, and, indeed exploited such protectors to advance their careers or general condition in life. The French courtesan Marie Duplessis did it so well before she died at age 23 that she became immortalized in Degas's lifetime as a Dumas protagonist in print and a Verdi heroine on stage. Mathilde Kschessinska, Imperial Russia's most famous ballerina, secured the romantic patronage of the future Tsar Nicholas II and then moved on to two Romanov Grand Dukes, eventually settling down with one of them after an unmatched career at the height of her art form. But the presenters here would deny such women any agency, badly needing them, even at the height of fame and success, to be victims. No one viewing this colorful but misleading exhibition should believe they were.

The Violent Bear It Away:
Flannery O'Connor Gets Canceled

The great Southern author Flannery O'Connor has been resurrected from the dead to bring gender equity to the victims' roster of our current *jacquerie*, most of whose victims are of the white male category. In June 2020, liberal Catholic writer Paul Elie, a fellow of my nominally Catholic alma mater, Georgetown University, published a preachy article in the *New Yorker* titled "How Racist Was Flannery O'Connor?" (answer: somewhat racist), alerting the world that the celebrated writer, who died in 1964, shockingly failed to live up to the standards of the modern progressive left. Elie suggested that if we have pure consciences of the type of which undoubtedly pristine *New Yorker* contributors might today approve, we should reexamine O'Connor's "racist passages" regardless of context and "face them squarely" in our own mandatory intellectual struggle sessions with hypocrisy. His evidence for her retrograde speech and attitudes has long been known. It includes now-objectionable language expressed in the 1940s, when O'Connor was a teenage girl, but has been reinforced recently by the publication of previously unpublished private correspondence in a volume called *Good Things Out Of Nazareth.*

We can only imagine how many lonely and spiritually empty woksters desperate to conform to a secular faith based on guilt purged their volumes of O'Connor's collected works while "decolonizing" their Ikea bookshelves. But Elie's article provoked ire at Maryland's Loyola University, a once respectable Jesuit institution sharing O'Connor's Catholic faith that named a student residence hall after her in 2007. Homebound students who may have glanced through their suburban parents' back issues of the *New Yorker* seem to have caught wind of her thoughtcrime from perusing Elie's article and drafted a brief but bizarre online petition worth repeating full:

> Recent letters and postcards written by Flannery O'Connor express strong racist sentiments and hate speech. Her name and legacy should not be honored nor glorified [*sic*] on our Evergreen Campus.

"*Recent* letters and postcards?" One does not need a Jesuitically-trained mind to reason that someone who has been cold in the ground for more than half a century has not written anything "recent," objectionable or otherwise. It seems well within reason to surmise that the petitioners, who are, after all, products of woefully (wokefully?) deficient American humanities education, simply have no idea who Flannery O'Connor was and believe that she is a living individual of racist proclivities spouting offensive statements that they did not have the time or attention span to look up and include. The grammatical error in the petition's second sentence suggests that these poorly educated youths could learn a thing or two from the eloquent economy of her prose rather than consign her to the dustbin on the basis of a sententious article by a pompous guilty white man in a dreary publication whose cartoons have long since ceased to be funny.

Be that as it may, the Elie-inspired petition attracted over a thousand signatures. Loyola's Jesuit president Father Brian Linnane, who may be Catholic, soon caved in what he described as a "difficult" decision, while nevertheless acknowledging that in O'Connor's fiction "the dignity of African American persons and their worth is consistently upheld, with the [white] bigots being the object of ridicule." Father Brian announced the immediate renaming of O'Connor Hall for Sister Thea Bowman, a Mississippi-born granddaughter of slaves who was the first African-American to join the Franciscan Sisters of Perpetual Adoration, and who is now under consideration for canonization in Rome.

Father Brian also announced a new commission that will comprehensively study Loyola's honorific naming practices to root out any sign of ideological impurity, perhaps ignorant of the fact that French revolutionaries did the same thing with equal zeal to Catholic sites in the shadow of a device that removed the heads of thousands of his fellow clergymen. While Father Brian's assessment of O'Connor's fiction is correct, his logic suggests that even Martin Luther King could be struck down from honorary naming. The great civil rights leader did, after all, both advocate for African-American dignity and use the hated "n-word" in his *Letter From A Birmingham Jail*. Indeed, a hapless university lecturer in California was recently investigated by his institution for reading King's letter, "n-word" and all, aloud in a classroom.

But like so much of this recent unpleasantness, the issue is not one of logic or even power but of image, the major concern of all university presidents, whose worth is no longer measured by intellectual leadership but by fundraising ability and attendant public relations management. Father Brian clearly has no desire to be seen as even remotely tolerating ambiguous racism of three generations ago and threw one of America's greatest women writers – and a disabled one at that – posthumously under the bus to look woke enough to avoid being called out by his university's inarticulate but tuition-paying adolescents lest they mar his august leadership with something so unseemly as a campus protest.

Not all may be lost, however. The superb O'Connor specialist Angela Alaimo O'Donnell, a former Loyola faculty member now at Fordham University, who wrote the definitive book on O'Connor and race, has penned a letter that has been signed by more than eighty scholars and clergymen urging a reversal of Father Brian's shallow capitulation to an online mob. Among them is the celebrated African-American novelist Alice Walker, who in a separate missive poignantly urged us to "honor Flannery for growing," to use her legacy – warts and all – to teach, and to observe the danger of a slippery slope that could consign virtually any great cultural figure of the past to oblivion by applying the modern standards of a small but unfortunately vocal segment of what passes for our intelligentsia. There was no online counterpetition, but Loyala did was hold a handful of webinars to discuss the issue with leading scholars. O'Donnell was not one of them.

Vive Le Roi!:
St. Louis Refuses to Cancel St. Louis

White males are unpopular in America these days, especially if they are dead and commemorated by a statue. Three years ago, in simpler times, it was only Confederate Civil War heroes who faced the opprobrium of *Das Woke Volk*. In the latest bout of iconoclasm, however, their statues' fate has been shared by almost anyone out of the past even tangentially connected to the suppression of people of color. George Washington and Thomas Jefferson? Slave owners, tear them down. Christopher Columbus? Never actually reached any part of what is now the continental United States, but explored the Caribbean, where Spain later introduced slavery, so down with him. Ulysses S. Grant? Led the Union armies to defeat the reviled Confederacy and later prosecuted the Ku Klux Klan, but his in-laws owned slaves and are believed to have given him one, whom he then freed. Tough call, but not in San Francisco, where an angry mob toppled his statue. Abraham Lincoln? Famously freed the slaves, but may have spoken disparagingly of them. Vandalize the tall, stovepipe-hat wearing bastard! Jimi Hendrix? Who knows, but he did play the now-criticized American national anthem at Woodstock fifty years ago ... and in those benighted times of peace and love no one found the courage to say a thing. Get him!

Who knows where it will end, but even non-Americans of yesteryear who failed to live up to the standards of modern progressive left are now liable to censure. As the Indian (but not the American) media has widely reported, Gandhi's statue in central Washington, DC was vandalized and had to be covered in plastic wrap. Saint Junipero Serra, a Spanish priest who ministered in California long before it became American, fell alongside General Grant in San Francisco. In the early days of the recent iconoclasm, protesters in Louisville, Kentucky damaged a statue of Louis XVI, the ill-fated monarch dethroned by the French Revolution, who is nevertheless remembered with gratitude by Americans for France's military contributions in the War of Independence.

It is Louis XVI's antecedent Louis IX (reigned 1226-1270), however, who has now been targeted for purposeful destruction in this American *jacquerie*. Emboldened by the recent removal of a local Columbus statue, organizers of an internet petition signed by nearly a thousand people have called for the city of St. Louis, Missouri not merely to remove a bold bronze equestrian statue of him that stands in the city's Forest Park, but also to rename the city altogether, "to something more suitable and indicative of our values." Unfortunately for humorists, no suggestions were made.

On June 27, about two hundred militant anti-Louis protesters assembled before the saintly monarch's statue, facing off against a determined band of counterprotesters, mainly Catholics led by a local priest, Father Stephen Schumacher, who led them in praying the rosary for a king who was canonized for his immense acts of charity for the poor and sick of his realm. A police line separated the two camps, but some of the statue's defenders were nevertheless violently assaulted. Unfortunately for proponents of law and order, no arrests were made.

Those who grew up in America when history was still taught in our country may remember that St. Louis, which lies west of the mighty Mississippi River, was originally a French settlement founded in 1764 by fur traders as a commercial outpost connecting the continental interior with the Spanish Southwest over land and, via New Orleans, with the rest of the world. They named it after the saintly king from their country's storied past, the patron saint of their reigning monarch Louis XV, and the name stuck after a frustrated Napoleon sold the vast Louisiana Territory (named for another Louis – the XIV in this case) to the United States in 1803. As the city's trading importance faded, it assumed a new role as a gateway for settlers heading West.

Louis IX's statue dates from a later era, when the city of St. Louis, in a sign of the tolerant internationalism we are now all supposed to embrace, hosted the 1904 World's Fair, immortalized in the 1944 film *Meet Me in St. Louis*. Officially known as *The Apotheosis of St. Louis*, the statue was a temporary plaster structure that greeted visitors at the fair's entrance. The bronze replica recently in contention was installed in the city's Forest Park two years later, in 1906. Louis IX's iconic profile became part of the city's iconography, remaining an unofficial symbol until the unique Gateway Arch, a stylized structure of rising nearly 200 meters high to celebrate the settlement of the American West, opened in 1965 (no protests against it yet, despite the ill treatment of Native Americans during the Western settlement).

Apart from Louis IX's gender and skin color, what was the offence of this medieval ruler, the only King of France ever to be canonized? He died in 1270, long before there was an "n-word" for him to use had he spoken English, a language that did not then exist in modern form. According to the poorly written petition to remove his statue, however, he was "a rabid anti-semite [*sic*] who spearheaded many persecutions against the Jewish people." "Centuries later," it continues in a fanciful adaptation of the historical record, "Nazi Germany gained inspiration and ideas from Louis IX as they [*sic*] embarked on a campaign of murderous genocide against the Jewish people. Louis IX was also vehemently Islamophobic and led a murderous crusade against Muslims." For the organizers of this odd campaign, "it's an outright disrespect [*sic*] for those who are part of these faith communities to have to live in a city named after a man committed to the murder of their co religionists [*sic*]." Why the organizers "have to live" in a place with a name they find objectionable is not clear, but their point of view very much is.

The proposition that a foreign ruler whose reign ended 750 years ago in another country inspires racial hatred in America today would be too ridiculous to merit comment were the threat to America's heritage – be it of an important city's founding by pioneering migrants or of the inclusive World's Fair that later celebrated global diversity – not so violently serious. Of course there is no indication that the French fur traders invoked Louis IX to scare and oppress Muslim and Jewish populations that did not exist in the primordial wilderness of the eighteenth-century North American Midwest. Nor is there any evidence that putting up a commemorative statue of the city's namesake over a century ago – to greet visitors to an avowedly internationalist World's Fair, no less, was conceived with malice and bigotry toward anyone.

Happily, the anti-Louis crowd did not get its way. Nearly 6,000 people have signed a counterpetition calling for the statue to be left alone.

The Islamic Foundation of Greater St. Louis issued a statement that disparaged the movement to remove the statue, arguing instead that present-day collaborations between faith communities "can help us move forward." The Catholic Archdiocese of St. Louis complemented that sentiment stating, "St. Louis is an example of an imperfect man who strived to live a life modeled after the life of Jesus Christ. For St. Louisans, he is a model for how we should care for our fellow citizen." Less pleasantly, a couple of days later a different group of protesters marching in St. Louis found themselves on the wrong end of firearms aimed at them by a middle-aged white couple – substantial Democratic Party campaign contributors, it turned out – who claim to have felt threatened by the protesters and have justified their actions by invoking Missouri's not inappositely named "castle doctrine," which allows the use of deadly force to protect private property. Their leftist politics notwithstanding, they became Fox News heroes, were invited to Trump reelection campaign events, and spoke at the 2020 Republican National Convention. The husband of the couple is now running to be a Republican candidate for Senate.

A simpler statement in this Middle American mess came from one of the counterprotesters, for whom Louis IX "symbolizes deep faith and convictions." "I stand for him," she said, "and I stand for those Catholic virtues and those Catholic values that I think are important, like courage, faith, and love." Those values are by no means limited to Catholics, but if all Americans could embrace them, they may yet find themselves blessed with hope as well.

Get Woke and Go Broke:
The High Price of Canceling
James Levine at the Metropolitan Opera

The pandemic has been a financial disaster for arts institutions worldwide, but nowhere more than in New York, where early local government mismanagement resulted in a disproportionately high number of cases and deaths, and drove many of the city's arts patrons and high-value taxpayers into refuges elsewhere. The Metropolitan Opera, the city's premiere performing company, lost an estimated $60 million from the cancelation of its remaining 2019-2020 season and as much as another $200 million in 2020-2021, which was canceled in its entirety.

How sad, then, that just before this fiscal tsunami swept down the already struggling opera company had to reach a legal settlement with arguably the single most important performer in its history, former music director and celebrated conductor James Levine. Levine, who debuted at the Met in 1971 and went on to revolutionize the company's performance standards, among many other artistic achievements around the world, was suspended without pay in December 2017 amid revelations of decades-old sexual harassment claims and then, in March 2018, fired him from his post as music director emeritus and all other responsibilities.

Almost immediately following Levine's suspension, but months before the Met's internal investigation reached any conclusions, the Met's general manager Peter Gelb publicly stated that "this is a tragedy for anyone whose life had been affected," as though the allegations were already proved true. All American arts institutions with ties to Levine categorically severed relations with him, with Puritanical Boston's symphony, which he led from 2004 to 2011, declaring that Levine would never again work with it, presumably even if he had been found innocent.

Much of the media all but declared Levine's guilt, smugly citing Gelb's statement along with other gossip that led one to wonder how the pundits would have reacted if mere innuendo had superseded the laws and contracts governing *their* employment. Levine's publisher withdrew a lucrative book contract. Banal *New York Times* music critic Anthony Tommasini sniffed that he would no longer keep Levine-led recordings in his living room, where Manhattan's moral guardians might disapprovingly glimpse them at some insipid cocktail party. The Met's Sirius radio channel for a time stopped broadcasting performances Levine had conducted in past decades, diminishing the quality of its content and inflicting unwarranted collateral damage on the hundreds of other performers featured in them, who had nothing at all to do with the situation.

Levine denied the allegations from the start, and within days of his termination filed a lawsuit against the Met for breach of contract, and against the Met and Gelb for defamation, along with other claims. He sought over $5.8 million in damages, mainly for lost income. His case was compelling. No allegation against him has ever been proved or found factual, in a court of law or otherwise. To the contrary, police investigations of his alleged conduct, including one that the Met knew about as long before the scandal as October 2016, identified no grounds even to charge him with any crime, let alone convict him of one.

Levine's court complaint, which is available in the public record, identified a substantial amount of countervailing evidence, including years of friendly correspondence from his alleged victims long after he had allegedly abused them. No allegation involved any form of penetrative sex, which is more than both major political parties' 2020 presidential candidates can say about the allegations against them. Even if this and similar behavior rose to what some considered to be sexual harassment by the standards of 2017 (which are already markedly different from those of 2021), Levine's contract contained no "morals clause" that might have given the company grounds to fire him for merely causing it embarrassment short of legal transgression. The Met's official statement on his dismissal only claimed that its internal investigation had found "credible evidence that Mr. Levine engaged in sexually abusive and harassing conduct towards vulnerable artists in the early stages of their careers." Unsupported by any disclosed evidence, that very statement formed the basis of one of Levine's defamation claims.

With the allegations arriving in the hysterical atmosphere that shook the entertainment world in the weeks after the revelations against Harvey Weinstein, the Met stuck to its guns over the Levine allegations, supported by a wide swath of opinion willing to toss overboard a thousand years of basic legal protections on the ever less compelling premise that individuals who complain of sexual harassment never lie unless they are accusing Joe Biden.

The Met filed a countersuit against Levine for an amount identical to his relief claim, arguing without much evidence that his alleged actions had resulted in actionable damages, and disclosed details of some of the allegations. The Met's lawyers eventually convinced a judge to dismiss most of Levine's defamation claims, but perhaps the most important one – his objection to the Met's statement that there was "credible evidence" against him – was allowed to proceed along with his other claims. Along the way, the company disposed of the octogenarian director John Copley over an allegedly "inappropriate" comment to a member of the Met's chorus. Later it removed tenor Vittorio Grigolo from its roster over an alleged incident of unwelcome touching during a curtain call while he was performing with another opera company in Japan, and, after some clumsy hesitation undoubtedly informed by the corrective of Levine's lawsuit, secured the departure of operatic superstar Plácido Domingo over allegations of long past misconduct involving his work at other opera companies.

After months of further legal wrangling, in August 2019 the parties in Levine's case reached a settlement. The terms were subject to a non-disclosure agreement. Both sides stayed tightlipped, making the settlement details the best kept secret in the performing arts universe for more than a year and engendering an enormous amount of speculation about even whether any money had changed hands.

We now know that money did, indeed, change hands. According to at least two internal sources cited by the *New York Times* on September 21, 2020, the date that would have been the opening night of the Met's season had it been held, Levine got $3.5 million, or about 60 percent of the damages demanded in his lawsuit. This sizeable payment strongly suggests what many have long suspected – that the Met's "credible evidence" was probably far less than "credible," and that the company was unwilling to risk an expensive and humiliating loss at trial, where its officials and Levine's accusers would have to have repeated their stories under oath.

The woke world is saddened by the results. The *New York Times's* story, by classical music writer Michael Cooper and, for some reason, James B. Stewart, author of a recent book called *Deep State: Trump, the FBI, and the Rule of Law*, scolds its readers under the facile title, "The Met Opera Fired James Levine, Citing Sexual Misconduct. He Was Paid $3.5 Million." Noting the Met's already ailing finances, the story's authors mourn that "now the company is fighting for its survival," in part, they imply, because Levine had the poor manners to assert his contractual and employment rights rather than meekly accept ignominious cancelation after a stellar fifty-year career.

Levine's payoff equaled only about two percent of the Met's projected losses from March to December 2020, but even if it were consequential enough to imperil the company's future, its board, management, patrons, audience, employees, artists, and media sympathizers might better ask why it so recklessly denied due process, especially to a celebrity employee with the substantial means necessary to bring down the cold hand of the law. But rather than raise that obvious question as #MeToo fades into #SoWhat, Cooper and Stewart tried to find irony in Levine's post-cancelation professional future, which to their apparent bemusement included an engagement to conduct Berlioz's *La Damnation de Faust* in Florence in January 2021.[3] Whose souls are for sale?

---

[3] The continuing pandemic caused those performances to be canceled. Levine then died on March 9, 2021.

Section III:
Entertainment

Cancel HBO:
The New Censorship Comes For HBO

After the national race riots that followed the horrific death of George Floyd, hosts of wokevolk emerged to exploit the racially charged atmosphere to resume purging American culture to their liking. Remaining Confederate monuments have been toppled through means legal and illegal, while a fair number of statues of other white males on the nasty order of George Washington and Abraham Lincoln are under threat. The United States Navy and Marine Corps, and even NASCAR, have all banned the Confederate battle flag. The airing of dissenting opinions about how to handle the recent unrest has led to the swift ouster of major media figures whose broadmindedness is thought to have posed "danger" to their staff. Everyone else has been put on notice that merely failing to voice support for woke directives is an act of aggression. "Silence," one common slogan succinctly puts it, "is Violence."

As companies big and small rush to be on the "right side of history," HBO Max removed the classic 1939 film *Gone With The Wind* from its new streaming service. Simply by having been a "product of its time" the 81-year old film set in and around Atlanta, which was again recently on fire, unpardonably sinned because it "depicts some of the ethnic and racial prejudices that have, unfortunately, been commonplace in American society."

This censorious decision against a film that produced the first Academy Award bestowed on an African-American artist (Hattie McDaniel won for Best Supporting Actress) came down just three days after John Ridley, the director of the bludgeoning *12 Years A Slave*, demanded *Gone With The Wind's* removal in a *Los Angeles Times* op-ed. Ridley declaimed that it "glorifies the antebellum south. It is a film that, when it is not ignoring the horrors of slavery, pauses only to perpetuate some of the most painful stereotypes of people of color." Made more than eight decades ago, *Gone With The Wind* appallingly fails to meet Ridley's expectations today.

To add insult to injury, Ridley continued, it did not even have a warning or disclaimer to spare the delicate sensitivities of people who might unwittingly be exposed to the horror of Vivien Leigh but could blithely watch the looting of Lower Manhattan or violent seizure of downtown Seattle on every news channel. Ridley assured the reader that he does not "believe in censorship" – except when he does – and that he only wants to "make the world a better place" by using his celebrity to control what his fellow citizens may or may not view in their own homes via an optional media service for which they have paid. The CEO of HBO Max's parent company, a man who will not go down in the annals of free expression, described the decision to remove the film as a "no-brainer."

Given the nature of the invective, one could be forgiven for wondering whether any of *Gone With The Wind*'s cancelers has ever actually watched the film, especially in an era when millennials – who dominate streaming service usage – lack the time, interest, or attention span to sit through an old movie that clocks in at nearly four hours. Indeed, more than 75 percent of millennials surveyed in 2017 reported never having seen *any* film made in the 1940s or 1950s, let alone in the 1930s.

Education has not and is unlikely to remedy the situation. Screening *Gone With The Wind* has long been taboo on American campuses, where freedom of speech and expression are now themselves fading memories of a bygone age. When National Public Radio's insipid *All Things Considered* program departed from its usual wallpaper paste-dull content to research a story on the film on the occasion of its seventy-fifth anniversary in 2014, it confirmed that many of its ostensibly well-educated younger staffers had, in fact, never seen it.

Their blistering ignorance was shared by a film class at Washington's prestigious Georgetown University (my alma mater), in which most of the students confessed to NPR that they had not seen it, either. This did not stop them from having opinions about it, however. As one of these best and brightest of young American scholars so eloquently put it, "Everything I've seen about it says it, like, glorifies the slave era ... and I dunno, what's the point of that? I don't see that as a good time in history ... like, oh, sweet, a love story of people who own slaves." (Even that dull witted observation is inaccurate: Rhett Butler is not a slaveowner, while Scarlett O'Hara's father owns the family's slaves, not she). Ridley's complaint that simply seeing *Gone With The Wind* listed among hundreds of other films on HBO Max was so "painful" that he wrote an open letter to major newspaper demanding its removal suggests that he himself may never have found the intestinal fortitude to sit through it all.

Does *Gone With The Wind* really "glorify" the slave era and the Old South that was defined by it? For those vast multitudes who have not seen the film, it is a tempestuous love story set against the backdrop of that world's total destruction during and after the American Civil War. At the time it was made, it was as far removed in time from that conflict as we are now removed from World War II. The film shows no heroic battle scenes, but rather devastated landscapes, long casualty lists, an epic panorama shot showing a sprawling field of ill cared for Confederate wounded, and, mercifully in the shadows, a horrific leg amputation conducted without anesthetic. It makes no heroic statement about the antebellum South and its fate, but fits neatly within the pacifist ethos of the interwar era in which it was made, in which a solid 75 percent of Americans opposed any involvement in the world war that broke out that same year.

Within the first thirty minutes, the film's rebellious anti-hero Rhett Butler condemns the imminent war as hopeless folly to a large gathering of headstrong Southern gentlemen. His opinion is so unpopular that he is nearly challenged to a duel. Almost all of those present who are identified by name later die inglorious offscreen deaths while their splendorous surroundings lie in the path of Sherman's devastating March to the Sea.

Rhett spends the rest of the film, even when romancing the vain and narcissistic Scarlett O'Hara – who refers to plantation life as "Hell," – mocking the very "Cause" that so many of today's woke warriors hate, along with all of the old South's other social conventions.

The survivors are condemned to squalor, with Scarlett reduced to eating raw turnips while her sisters callous their hands picking cotton and her once proud but now insane father clutches worthless Confederate war bonds. She rebuilds the family's blighted fortunes through hardnosed entrepreneurship in the commercial economy, doing business with the northern occupiers and employing not recently emancipated slaves but less expensive white convict laborers. Her crush Ashley Wilkes, the son of a neighboring plantation owner, opposes war in all its forms, abhors slavery, and we learn, planned to free his family's slaves upon inheriting them had the Civil War not intervened.

While slavery is depicted in the film, nothing in it suggests that it was good or anything to be missed. The film's vilest character by far is the O'Hara's overseer, an unscrupulous Northerner, whom we first meet when Mrs. O'Hara disdainfully informs him of the death of his newborn child by a poor local girl he had impregnated and abandoned. The last time we see him, now a carpetbagger using his new allegiance to torment his former employers, Scarlett throws a fistful of dirt in his face after he tries to bully the impoverished O'Haras into selling him their family home at a cut rate, deriding them in the process for being Irish. Even the O'Haras' slaves look down on this miscreant throughout the film as "no-count white trash."

Even if the casual observer still thinks this ceaseless stream of death and degradation glorifies the antebellum American South, *Gone With The Wind* does not end at all happily. Rhett and Scarlett marry after she survives two lesser husbands whom she uses rather than loves, but their only child dies young in a horrible riding accident, her life cut short by the same cavalier horsemanship that defined a vanished culture of equestrian gentility. Still obsessed with Ashley, Scarlett drives the exasperated Rhett to leave, famously telling her that he "frankly" does not "give a damn" about her fate. Abandoned to her neuroses, she is trapped between an irretrievable past and an uncertain future.

This melodrama is hardly the stuff of glory. It is hard to imagine a militia band of even the most determined white nationalists using the film to inculcate racist values in the future builders of a white ethnostate, or anyone else viewing it as anything other than epic fantasy set in a universe that could no longer exist. Its popularity has never been in doubt. A smash hit upon release, it remained the top selling American film until *The Godfather* displaced it in the 1970s, and, adjusted for inflation, it has been rated the highest grossing film of all time. When it was first televised in 1976, an estimated 47 percent of American households tuned in. When

Turner Classic Movies premiered in 1994, it was the first film broadcast on the network, which still regularly broadcasts today along with other films that might not be considered politically correct. According to a 2014 poll, 73 percent of Americans who had seen *Gone With The Wind* – and, ironically given the current context, an identical 73 percent of *black* Americans who had seen it – rated it "good," "very good," or "one of the best" films ever made.

After a well justified and encouragingly effective outcry, HBO Max returned the film to its service, albeit with "a discussion of its historical context and a denouncement" of its "objectionable" features in the hope that a preachy lecture to viewers will help "create a more just, equitable and inclusive future." Jacqueline Stewart, a University of Chicago film and media studies professor, provides this discussion. She has stated that *Gone With The Wind* should "stay in circulation and remain available for viewing," but mainly as "a prime text for examining expressions of white supremacy in popular culture."

Disturbed by the film's failure to show a sufficient amount of black suffering, her goal is to warn those who choose to watch it against "false pedigrees" with glamorous Southern aristos whose haughty bearing could deceive "working class and poor white viewers" from forming "beneficial alliances with their Black working class and poor counterparts." Her fundamental goal is to transform an undisputed American classic into material for "re-education," a term rarely associated with any democratic society. HBO Max's executives may have imagined this light form of Maoism as a good marketing ploy or at least as a way to avoid being condemned for "silence." Either way, until this incident I had never heard of their service, though news of HBO's weak financial situation soon emerged. Now I have a reason not to subscribe to it.

Disclaimer:
Mel Brooks is Canceled

No sooner had HBO Max, the financially troubled American cable television network's new film streaming service, signaled its virtue by removing *Gone With The Wind* from viewing so that the classic film could be properly "contextualized" than attention fell on Mel Brooks's smash hit 1974 comedy *Blazing Saddles*. Added to HBO Max's streamed offerings since the *Gone With The Wind* dust up and known for its liberal use of the feared and loathed "n-word," *Blazing Saddles* arrived with a similarly patronizing disclaimer already installed. In a three-minute introduction that apparently cannot be skipped over, film professor Jacqueline Stewart is there again, this time to inform viewers that "racist language and attitudes pervade the film," while instructing them that "those attitudes are espoused by characters who are portrayed here as explicitly small-minded, ignorant bigots ... The real, and much more enlightened, perspective is provided by the main characters played by Cleavon Little and Gene Wilder."

Thanks, Aunt Jacqueline. If you have not seen *Blazing Saddles* – and if you are under the age of 40 there is an excellent chance some priggish authority figure sanitized it out of your cosseted millennial existence – it stands as one of the greatest, and the certainly the funniest, *anti-racist* films of all time. Based on a story by Andrew Bergman, Brooks conceived it as a scathing send-up of racism and the hypocrisy that still enabled it after the great civil rights victories of the 1960s. Brooks's idiom was a parody of the classic Western, by then an exhausted genre that had, among other flaws, become inanely predictable and was much criticized for leaving out minorities and questions of race. A landmark of American film, *Blazing Saddles* was selected in 2006 for inclusion in the U.S. National Film Registry, which recognizes "culturally, historically, or aesthetically significant films" worthy of preservation.

Drenched in hilarity – and by my count using the "n-word" 17 times in its 93-minute run – the plot involves a conspiracy by an avaricious U.S. state attorney general who wants to drive white settlers off land he needs to complete a profitable railroad project. After having outlaws wreak mayhem on the townspeople, he recommends that the governor appoint a black sheriff to restore law and order, cynically assuming that their racism will cause them to reject the new lawman and give up. Despite a rough initial reception, the sheriff outwits attempts to get rid of him and, with the help of a washed up but sympathetic alcoholic gunslinger, leads the townspeople to victory, winning their love and respect before moving on to other brave deeds.

While HBO no longer wants to risk having its paying customers think for themselves (and what stale corporate outfit uneasily transitioning to a crowded new medium wouldn't?), it could rightly be said that anyone dumb enough to miss the film's message might be a recent product of American higher education.

I do not mean that at all facetiously. Decaying and run by a self-important clerisy whose demands to be taken seriously only become shriller as it declines in reach and vitality – and from which any participant can be dismissed for even the slightest speech or behavioral infraction – academia naturally discourages humor. Jokes, which can almost always cause some kind of offense, are simply too risky to be told or laughed at, even in private. Finding the wrong thing funny can invite career-hobbling accusations that one has demeaned a student or colleague and thereby made them feel unacceptably "uncomfortable" or even physically "unsafe." Perceived flippancy bruises sanctified "professional seriousness" in a way tantamount to sacrilege, and any amount of it diminishes the authority of the institutions and functionaries handing down our new mores. The only tolerated exceptions are a kind of solemn irony that offers comfort in coping with academia's increasing irrelevance and a resigned gallows humor about its ever more limited prospects for all but an ever smaller circle of the elect few.

Brooks's explosive mix of satire, sarcasm, and absurdity is not only toxic in such an environment but also requires levels of abstract and critical thought that our administrative-managerial caste would prefer us not to have, leaving it to assume that someone like Jacqueline Stewart has to explain the film to us in black and white (pun intended) terms.

This is not entirely new. Brooks's first film, *The Producers*, which satirizes Nazism, was shunned by all major movie studios and had to be released as an independent art film. When Warner Brothers screened *Blazing Saddles* prior to its release, one executive was so worried about its content that he wanted to withhold it from distribution and take a financial loss. The studio chief relented, but ordered Brooks to remove all uses of the "n-word," a directive he refused to follow. As recently as 2017, Brooks, by then a 91-year old American icon reasonably safe from cancelation, lamented that his film could not be made today because of our "stupidly politically correct" society, which he understandably believes has "killed comedy."

From a "woke" point of view, the "n-word" is hardly the film's only problem. Its "racist language and attitudes" extend to Mexicans, Chinese, Native Americans, Germans, Arabs, Jews, and the Irish. Brooks's cameo appearance in full Indian dress while speaking Yiddish suggests "cultural appropriation" of a magnitude that would get him expelled from Yale on any given Halloween. The governor's lascivious relationship with his sexpot secretary lightheartedly approaches what some joyless, passion-starved diversity bureaucrat would condemn as sexual harassment. The film seeks further taboo levity in drug abuse, capital punishment, physical and mental disabilities, cruelty to animals, and farting. Its climactic battle between the townspeople and outlaws spills into a modern studio rehearsal of stereotyped gay dancers practicing a routine called the French Mistake, an old slang term for when a heterosexual man "accidentally" wanders into same-sex relations.

HBO clearly cares above all about the racial issue, which in the current moment is the most visible and reliable lever to establish media mechanisms for thought control, and to condition mass acceptance of diminished rights of free speech and expression. There are hopeful signs that it will not succeed. In her bland moralizing tone, Stewart sounds like a Soviet bureaucrat of the late 1980s cataloguing the ideological demerits of some tentatively allowed item of Western culture to a jaded young audience ready to embrace it as enthusiastically as my university students did when I covertly screened *Blazing Saddles* for them after Gene Wilder's death in 2016. In that moment I did, indeed, scurry around after hours like a harried Czechoslovakian dissident trying to evade the authorities on his way to an underground discussion of John Stuart Mill. Perhaps not accidentally, when the HBO story broke it was one of my students who alerted me.

I am quite certain that I was the last university professor ever to show *Blazing Saddles* on a campus, but Stewart's tedious social justice blandishments do oddly fit with the film in at least one way. Early on, when outlaws are beating up an old lady while terrorizing the town, she looks to the camera and asks the viewer, "Have you ever seen such cruelty?" It is not hard to imagine, perhaps after a libation or two, even the stiff and sanctimonious Jacqueline Stewart turning to ask a captive HBO Max subscriber to equally comedic effect, "Have you ever seen such racism?"

One, Two, Three … Your Freedom Is Not Free:
Cancel Culture Comes For Dr. Seuss

"You will not, will not find him in a box. You will not, will not listen to him on Fox," might be a worthy Seussian rhyme for yet another culture war's recent *épopée*. Earlier this month, Dr. Theodor Seuss Geisel, creator of *The Cat in the Hat* and the whole universe of amusing books that helped teach generations of children to read, disappeared from the annual presidential address marking "Read Across America Day." Since 1998, this quasi-holiday has been sponsored every March 2, the day of Geisel's birth, by the major teacher's union, the National Education Association (NEA), apparently to remind us that American public schools remain so horribly deficient that they need a special day to encourage basic literacy.

About 80 years ago, Geisel, which no one else in the commentariat seems to realize is the German word for "scourge," committed the cardinal offense of drawing mildly racist cartoons of our World War II enemies while we were fighting them in a war that they started in an especially nasty way. He also drew cartoon figures – in books of cartoons – that are allegedly so "hurtful and wrong" that in late 2020 his literary heirs quietly decided to remove six books he published decades ago from future publication. When they announced this on Read Across America Day 2021, prices for used copies skyrocketed on Ebay, with some vendors seeking to profit from the inevitable appeal of the forbidden by advertising them as "banned." Ebay has been compliantly cracking down on the ads, but they continue to pop up, often earning hundreds of dollars in intense bidding wars.

In these charged circumstances, Dr. Seuss can no longer be extolled by the White House and, per NEA mandate, he is to be deemphasized in schools observing Read Across America Day. In Loudon County, Virginia, a remote suburban area of Washington now densely settled by lower-end members of our managerial-administrative caste who cannot afford to live closer to the nation's capital, the school district issued a "guidance" that its minions "not connect Read Across America Day exclusively with Dr. Seuss' birthday" because "research in recent years has revealed strong racial undertones" in his *œuvre*.

The recent "research" cited by the Loudon County school district consists of one poorly written academic article that a social work graduate with no apparent humanities education and her graduate student husband published in an obscure journal edited by the aspiring social worker's cousin. They argued therein that Dr. Seuss is "Orientalist," "anti-black," and an agent of "white supremacy," and advocated his removal from Read Across America reading lists and replacement by unspecified "authors of color," apparently without regard for whether or not *their* content is racist.

Who knew? Surely not Cindy Lou Who, but like good Outer Party types who need to prove themselves in hope of climbing the bureaucratic ladder and maybe one day a Metro-convenient house in some dreary suburb closer to Washington, Loudon County schoolmarms dutifully marched along and made themselves into a national laughing stock. Within 24 hours, memes that may be hurtful, and possibly even wrong, cascaded over social media mocking the affair. Right-wing pundits wrote easy outrage copy, with even pious Never Trumpers straightening their bowties to take a rare stand. Mainstream media hacks have been admonishing them to focus on other problems lest voters who are already losing regard for Biden conclude that the Democratic Party is the party of banning books. The Loudon County school district issued a panicky corrective notice insisting that Dr. Seuss has not been "banned," but merely classified as a racist in a world where being called a racist is tantamount to being banned, canceled, fired, or otherwise outcast. Not even soft tyranny can withstand ridicule, but to keep those cancel-culture-killing memes flowing let us ask, "Do you like it, Sam-I-am?"

Moping About Muppets:
Another Humiliation for Disney

In our woke world, Disney it was perhaps inevitable that Disney would manage make itself look ridiculous before an ever warier public. This time its victim is *The Muppet Show*, a campy parody of variety programs featuring Jim Henson's beloved puppet figures, which were originally introduced on *Sesame Street*. It aired weekly on old-fashioned network television from 1976 to 1981. Evolving from *Sesame Street*, *The Muppet Show* combined its puppet characters' antics with witty word play and middle-brow entertainment acts to appeal to adults as well as children. On February 19, 2021, all five seasons dropped on the media giant's Disney Plus streaming service for new audiences to enjoy while fueling bouts of Generation X nostalgia for simpler times.

The Muppet Show's widened appeal is now its Achilles' heel. Before each episode, Disney has inserted a statement ritually confessing: "This program includes negative depictions and/or mistreatment of peoples or cultures. These stereotypes were wrong then and are wrong now. Rather than remove this content, we want to acknowledge its harmful impact, learn from it and spark conversation to create a more inclusive future together." A separate warning cautions that viewers will be exposed to "tobacco depictions," perhaps to prevent millennial snowflakes from running out of the room in horror when the aged comedian Milton Berle puffs on a cigar during his guest appearance.

Apart from the wincing misuse of the word "impact" when what I believe the author-commissar meant to write was "effect," Disney does not identify which "peoples" or "cultures" are depicted negatively or mistreated, or which "stereotypes" are and were "wrong." Are we supposed to watch all 120 or so episodes of all five seasons and guess? Might the list be too lengthy for an on-screen warning, and, if it is, why not just bury *The Muppet Show* altogether as an irredeemable artifact of pre-woke civilization, like so many offensively illustrated bottles of maple syrup or statues of Abraham Lincoln? Further, if *Muppet Show* stereotypes are "wrong," are there other stereotypes out there that are "correct?" And if there are, why are they not identified, and who decides which ones are acceptable and which are not?

Disney does not explain why *The Muppet Show* is so capable of causing such terrific "harm" that we must be warned in advance that puppets are about to perpetrate it. The warning's invitation to discuss how we might rely on the show's apparent failings to create a more "inclusive future" recalls the greatest unanswered questions of the woke movement – what would a future that is more "inclusive" look like, and how would it be different from the present? We are never told, here or anywhere else. Could it be that there is no substantive answer, and that our minders merely want the power to shape and condition our thoughts in a perpetual quest for an unobtainable heaven of utopian equality? Permanent control over how a society thinks has been a long-standing goal of the totalitarian mindset, yet no totalitarian has ever readily relinquished it once obtained.

From the woke perspective, a randomly selected first-season episode of *The Muppet Show* offers a cornucopia of aggressions both macro and micro. Our first potentially "wrong" stereotype is the Swedish chef – dumb, inept, incomprehensible, and ultimately violent, carrying on minstrel-like in an ersatz language mocking Swedish while flipping his pancakes so high that they stick to the ceiling and have to be brought down by gunfire. What a slur on the noble people of Sweden! It could uncomfortably remind those delicate Scandinavians that they have not fought a war for over two centuries are not particularly well known for their cuisine. And let us not forget their appalling treatment in classic Hollywood, where the playwright and screenwriter Maxwell Anderson dismissed their best and brightest star Ingrid Bergman as a "big, dumb, goddamn Swede!" Words hurt, and *The Muppet Show* should clearly have been more sensitive to the historical injustice of our society's rampant anti-Swedish oppression. Let us show solidarity in the face of their continuing humiliation.

In the same episode, we find the great triple threat of yesteryear Rita Moreno speaking with a Puerto Rican accent that was never her own. How traumatizing to see this obvious and insulting case of cultural appropriation so indifferently splayed across the screen! And there we have Miss Piggy – that porcine princess of privilege – mocking Moreno's appropriated accent with exaggerated rolls of the letter "r." Were the creators really so unaware of how very ostracizing and harmful it is to be mocked by a simulated pig? Clearly, they needed to be educated, and those who are left to shape the more "inclusive" future must maintain eternal vigilance against all pig-Latino hate speech.

White and class privilege also rear their ugly heads throughout the series. The otherwise innocuous-looking Scooter, a bespectacled novice who seems so nice and inoffensive in his casually preppy mien, sure does know how to get his way in the theater in which the show is set. All he has to do is issue implicit threats at Kermit the Frog, who manages the acts, by mentioning his unseen uncle, who owns the theater and will presumably wield all the inequitable power of finance capital if Scooter's whims and dictates are ignored. The hateful structures of power in the Muppet universe are all too obvious, even if their fetters are invisible.

And who could ignore Statler and Waldorf, the greatest villains of them all, a pair of old white males in black tie who survey the action from the elevated comfort of their exclusive box? Named for prominent hotels that are perhaps the source of their capitalistic wealth, their main function is to cast down sarcastic comments upon the poor defenseless performers while they also, to add insult to injury, mock each other for their various disabilities. At the very least, we should have a separate warning to guard us against the ugly and retrograde notion, so blatantly reinforced by *The Muppet Show*, that the arts only exist for the amusement and approval of rich old white men.

As the warning concludes, after viewing these historic crimes against wokeness, we might best report for reeducation at Disney's website, which offers a section called "Stories Matter." Illustrated with proud persons of color, it promises to "relentlessly champion the spectrum of voices and perspectives in our world." The Swedish chef will be marginalized no longer! Here he, and we, can indulge in an atmosphere "committed to stories with inspirational and aspirational themes" instead of idly laughing along in the shadow of outmoded and doomed hegemons like Statler and Waldorf. "Happily ever after doesn't just happen," Disney assures us in case anyone who has been conscious at any point over the past year remains unaware, "it takes effort. Effort we are making." How virtuous of them. But to what end?

Borat Bores Us:
Sacha Baron Cohen's Borat Sequel is a Flop

Two weeks before Amazon Prime's streaming service released the sequel to the comedian Sacha Baron Cohen's 2006 *Borat* film, or, to give the sequel its parodic full title, *Borat Subsequent Moviefilm: Delivery of Prodigious Bribe to American Regime for Make Benefit Once Glorious Nation of Kazakhstan*, he whined in his real voice to the few remaining adults who still read *Time* magazine that Facebook promotes information that the actor believes to be false, and that it refuses to adopt recommendations for "systemic reforms" (i.e. censorship) ominously demanded by a public interest group to which he belongs. His petulant article was illustrated by a photo of a young man in a mask marked "Covid-19 is a hoax."

A few days later, in a moment that strikingly resembled a *Borat* prank, Baron Cohen tweeted outrage upon learning that his plea for heightened Facebook censorship had itself been censored by Facebook, apparently for spreading false information. For one postmodern moment, none other than the creator of Borat languished as the publicly humiliated victim of his own "gotcha" form of humor. In ironic contrast to Kazakh public officials who have admitted that the first *Borat* film was funny and generated welcome curiosity about their country, Baron Cohen performed an entertaining parody of his actual self. One can almost imagine a bemused Borat mispronouncing the phrase "systemic reforms" in his mildly racist post-Soviet accent.

Baron Cohen may have spent the fourteen years between *Borats* indulging in the common Hollywood delusion that people will take even a dancing clown seriously if he made one funny film and several mediocre ones. That might pass muster in *Borat's* fictional Kazakhstan, which, we now learn, has a monkey who is both its Minister of Culture and leading porn star. Baron Cohen's real-life persona, however, appears to have all the levity of a Central Asian potassium factory and less self-awareness than his on-screen character showed when presenting gracious Southern dinner hosts with a plastic bag of his own excrement.

To be fair, sequels rarely do as well as any foundational film, and the first *Borat's* sheer bizarreness is no longer new or fresh. Baron Cohen can only be painfully aware of this after unsuccessful attempts to expand his impressions-and-mockery franchise in *Brüno* (2009) and *The Dictator* (2012), both of which were forgettable. He probably had no choice but to spend much of the *Borat* sequel in various disguises-over-his-disguise since the character's iconic appearance would have been too easily recognized. Dependent on fooling unsuspecting or, as often seems to be the case, misled Americans, the reprise suffered from Borat's lack of a self-contained universe akin to that of the Marx Brothers, the *Seinfeld* cast, or Larry David, where a continuity of character can roll forward without any concern about exhausting situational novelty.

Probably for that reason, the *Borat* sequel adheres formulaically to the first film. Once again, Borat is sent on a quest to faraway America to reach an inaccessible celebrity, this time tasked with gifting Kazakhstan's simian culture minister to Vice President Mike Pence. Borat's teenage daughter Tutar complicates things with her dream of being given away in an arranged marriage to a rich old man. She stows away in the monkey's shipping crate, eats him en route, and thereby forces her father to change his mission to give her to Mike Pence instead. Along the way, Borat's awkwardness and naïveté elicit what are supposed to be shocking admissions of prejudice and lunacy from mainly rural and Southern Americans. As in the first film, he embarrasses people in one-on-one meetings, behaves provocatively in confined public spaces, scandalizes an upper-class social affair, takes refuge with open-hearted but deeply flawed hosts who volunteer unsavory views, confronts pleasant elderly Jews with a caricatured mixture of fear and loathing, leads an offensive public sing-a-long, and infiltrates a mass event attended by people of whom Baron Cohen obviously disapproves. On the whole, it felt like a do-over but with the burden of a father-daughter drama that slows down the action without adding many laughs.

The sequel has some funny moments, but the culture has changed too drastically for it to enjoy anything like the first film's sensational popularity. Baron Cohen's humor lies in satirizing prejudices to ridicule people who hold or tolerate them. But in our post-satirical age, when the very concept of satire and the abstract thought it requires are so weakened that they now often need to be explained, his humor seems outdated and even superfluous. In a society largely captured by the new commonplace that all white people are racists, can revelations of casual prejudice still shock an audience widely trained to expect, expose, and even police it? Not really. Can a subject's racism still be in any way amusing if one accepts – nearly as an article of faith – that racism is the evil root cause of all human woe? Probably not. Censorious millennial viewers are more likely to track down and demand the sacking of the middle-aged bakery clerk who obligingly writes "Jews will not replace us" on Borat's cake than they are to laugh at her socially unconscious apathy. As long as two years before the sequel premiered, wokesters were already arguing that the racist, sexist, and homophobic stereotypes of Borat's vaguely Eurasian origins were unacceptable comedic material that have encouraged Westerners to demean peoples of the developing world. I doubt their sense of humor has much improved.

The film will also find little resonance with broad masses now terrorized by the notion that it is irredeemably wrong to cause any form of offence. In 2006, it was natural to take Borat's interview targets for simpletons and laugh at their foibles. Today's viewers, however, are far more likely to intuit that the targets' reputations and livelihoods depend on responding professionally to even the strangest and most impertinent situations, especially when they are aware that they are being filmed. A Georgia debutante coach who patiently explains that women are capable of doing many ordinary activities while menstruating, for example, is no longer merely the butt of a joke but a hostage to readily identifiable circumstances in which she could suffer serious consequences if she reacted differently. In a country where a significant percentage of the population knows that it can be publicly shamed, denied basic rights, and dismissed from employment for transgressing new speech and behavioral norms, these situational moments are much less mirthful to viewers.

The amplified power of social media also deflates this derivative sequel. When the original *Borat* film premiered, the first smart phones had just appeared, Facebook was in its infancy, and Twitter, Instagram, and other social media platforms offering instant photo and video sharing did not exist. In those halcyon days, it was easier for Baron Cohen to keep a lid on the behind-the-scenes preparation for his pranks, which consequently looked far more authentic. Now, even before the sequel's release, many have been breezily exposed as well orchestrated setups or near-setups. In the most famous example, the 76-year old presidential attorney Rudolph Giuliani is duped into giving a hotel suite interview to Tutar posing as an admiring professional journalist. She invites him into the suite's bedroom for a "sound check," where he proceeds to ask her for her personal contact information, recline on the bed, and put his hands in his trousers. Borat bursts in to tell him that at age fifteen Tutar is too old for him (the actress who plays Tutar is 24), causing Giuliani to storm out in distress.

This was clearly a very embarrassing moment for America's Mayor, a man who once prosecuted mafia bosses and led New York through 9/11 but is now reduced to claiming that he was only tucking in his shirt, an action I have never contemplated when reclining alongside a beautiful woman. He and Baron Cohen traded media barbs, with Donald Trump coming to Giuliani's assistance by calling Baron Cohen "unfunny" and a "creep" (They have a history – many years ago Trump walked out of a fake interview with Baron Cohen in his Ali G persona and later publicly called for him to be beaten up for a tasteless Academy Awards prank). The scene's editing leaves what really happened ambiguous, which is probably the best adjective to describe a film so out of step with our lamentable *Zeitgeist*.

Using the Force Against Wokeness:
A Galactic Scandal of Cancelation

"This is just the beginning ... welcome to the rebellion," tweeted the defiant American actress Gina Carano to her 860,000 followers the day after she learned from social media that she had been summarily fired from *The Mandalorian*, the Disney-produced *Star Wars* livestream series on which she played a recurring role. Over the past few months, Carano had racked up a long list of infractions that jeopardized her continuing employment, but, perhaps predictably in our neo-McCarthyite times, none of them had anything to do with how she did her job portraying a tough-as-nails mercenary who occasionally helps the show's star title character in his quest to deliver his young charge, "Baby Yoda," to the Jedi order.

Carano's transgression was to have the wrong political views. She expressed them on social media, in posts that questioned the validity of mail-in ballots in the 2020 presidential election and suggested that its results were fraudulent. She resisted calls to endorse the Black Lives Matter movement. She made a joke about people who wear more than one mask even as the pandemic wanes and an ever-rising percentage of Americans are now vaccinated. She failed to show mandatory solidarity with the transgendered community, to which she does not belong, by refusing to list pronouns that correspond to her gender identity. She even committed the cardinal sin of mocking the issue by listing her pronouns as "beep/bop/boop," the computerized sounds of a *Star Wars* droid.

These stands alone precipitated a sustained campaign to deny Carano continuing employment. The hashtag #FireGinaCarano illuminated the Twitter galaxy for months as the second season of her popular series was unveiled by Disney, which in 2012 purchased the *Star Wars* franchise from creator George Lucas for over $4 billion and proceeded to ruin it with a trilogy of poorly conceived sequels that replaced the original films' determined hero's quest to self-actualization with an awkward heroine's bumpy road to self-doubt and renunciation. Rumors held that fellow cast members had begun warning Carano about what she said on social media lest she rock the boat by indulging in her constitutionally protected freedom of expression.

Other chatter suggests that Disney effectively ordered her to apologize for offending the transgendered community and that she ruffled feathers by stopping short of such an apology to declare that she is not against that community. In December 2020, she was reportedly axed from a separate *Star Wars* spinoff, in which her *Mandalorian* character was supposed to star. On February 10, 2021, the final straw fell when the actress dared to suggest in an Instagram post that Americans like her were being persecuted for political reasons. She chose the charged metaphor of the Holocaust, which in addition to Jews, historically did include the Nazi persecution of individuals and groups for political reasons alone, including barring them from employment in the entertainment industry.

Within hours, Disney's Lucasfilm subsidiary announced that Carano would not return to work on *The Mandalorian* at any future time due to her purportedly "abhorrent and unacceptable" statement, which she had by then deleted. She was also dropped by her professional representative, United Talent Agency. Even the Hasbro toy company joined the mob and announced that it would no longer manufacture action figures of her *Mandalorian* character. On Ebay their expected scarcity has driven prices through the roof in intense bidding wars matched only by those for Dr. Seuss books. One optimistic vendor listed her *Mandalorian* action figure at $10,000. Lucasfilm later announced that Carano's fictional character, ironically a strong and fiercely independent woman who routinely bests lesser males in intense combat, will not be recast, meaning that she will simply disappear from the universe. Carano, it seemed, was canceled, erased, and unpersoned, not just in real-world professional life, but even in a shadow world of make-believe set a long time ago in a galaxy far, far away.

Or was she? Within 24 hours of Carano's cancelation, she re-emerged from what could only have been a very bad day to tell her fans: "I am sending out a direct message of hope to everyone living in fear of cancelation by the totalitarian mob. I have only just begun using my voice which is now freer than ever before, and I hope it inspires others to do the same. They can't cancel us if we don't let them."

Compare Carano's powerful and determined femininity – real, confident feminism, if you will – to the cringing self-abnegation of Chris Harrison, a gutless fraction of a man who was until recently presenter of ABC's reality series *The Bachelor*. A couple of days after Carano's cancelation, he got into trouble for defending a white female contestant who had attended a pre-Civil War-themed dress party long before anyone had heard of George Floyd. "I am deeply remorseful," Harrison whined on Instagram, "My ignorance did damage to my friends, colleagues, and strangers alike ... by excusing historical racism, I defended it. I invoked the term 'woke police,' which is unacceptable. I am ashamed over how uninformed I was. I was so wrong ... I am so grateful to those who reached out to help me on my path to anti-racism."

One could be forgiven for thinking he had danced a reel under the Confederate flag after watching an uncontextualized screening of *Gone With The Wind*. But we really should ask what "damage" was done to his friends, colleagues, and strangers by his purely verbal defense of a young woman who attended a private party of which he previously knew nothing. We might equally wonder why it is "unacceptable" to call people who surveil and punish others' speech in the name of what they describe as "wokeness" the "woke police," and who decided that they should have career-ending power over anyone in professional life. Nor is it clear why people should feel "ashamed" for being "uninformed." And should television presenters really only qualify for their jobs if they are treading a demonstrated "path to anti-racism?" Is just not being a racist insufficient? ("No," is the often repeated answer).

In his groveling penitence, Harrison sounds like a Stalinist purge victim confessing to anything and everything necessary to escape having a bullet fired into the back of his head in the hope that the Party might yet find a reduced but still productive use for him. Like those doomed Soviet ideologues, who were also almost never spared, it is likely that Harrison is dumb and desperate enough to believe in the unforgiving ideology behind the system that has destroyed him, and that he will continue to accept its chastisement in the impossible hope of redemption.

Gina Carano, however, angrily rejects that ideology and refreshingly seems never to have believed in it in the first place. This makes her strong in a society of weaklings. It gives her a future in which she can live, work, and even just be without the constant threat of being accused of offending the wrong person or media conglomerate. Her refusal to take the proverbial knee will allow her to thrive without what must be the exhausting anxiety of having her speech and behavior monitored by people vile and narcissistic enough to believe that her employment should depend on unswerving conformity to their politics. As she fully recognizes, she is a much freer person now than she was before.

Just as Carano released her hopeful statement, it was also announced that she will produce, direct, and star in a feature film in collaboration with conservative commentator Ben Shapiro, whose *Daily Wire* outfit has declared its intention to challenge Hollywood with an independent studio where performers are not punished for holding unfashionable views. That is a vaulting promotion from playing a recurring character on a streamed spinoff. Shapiro is happy to be working with a talented actress but added that he is "just as eager to show Hollywood that if they want to keep canceling those who think differently, they'll just be helping us build the Xwing to take down their Death Star." May the force be with them.

CPSIA information can be obtained
at www.ICGtesting.com
Printed in the USA
JSHW041954030322
23565JS00007B/156